What others are saying about
No More Lone Rangers:

"I believed in teams long before I stumbled and blundered my way into actually making them work in my youth ministry. This book could have saved me—and my ministry teammates—an awful lot of frustration. Thanks, Dave!"

> —**Dave Rahn,** *Director of Huntington College's Link Institute*
> *and Vice President of YFC/USA Ministries*

"Having helped train youth leaders for over twenty-five years, I can highly recommend this book. David gets it. He knows it's not about doing it alone or getting people to do what you want—it's about creating a team that frees people up to do ministry together. David offers practical and real-life help to do just that. He has been and still is in the trenches doing youth ministry in the real world, so you will see right away that what this book says rings true."

> —**Tic Long,** *President of Events, Youth Specialties*

"What I most appreciate about this book is the thorough care with which Dave Chow has woven together several different vital emphases: spiritual nurture, practical training, good recruitment, and community building. This is a careful and thoughtful work, and youth workers will find it to be very, very helpful."

> —**Duffy Robbins,** *Associate Professor of Youth Ministry,*
> *Eastern University*

"I have known Dave Chow for several years. He is a sensitive, intelligent practitioner of youth ministry. His book *No More Lone Rangers* reflects these qualities. He has done his homework. This is an extremely practical book in an easy-to-read format. This book would be a valuable asset to any youth minister's library."

> —**Dr. Les Christie,** *Chair of the Youth Ministry Department*
> *at San Jose Christian College*

Flagship church resources

from Group Publishing

Innovations From Leading Churches

Flagship Church Resources are your shortcut to innovative and effective leadership ideas. You'll find ideas for every area of church leadership, including pastoral ministry, adult ministry, youth ministry, and children's ministry.

Flagship Church Resources are created by the leaders of thriving, dynamic, and trend-setting churches around the country. These nationally recognized teaching churches host regional leadership conferences and are respected by other pastors and church leaders because their approaches to ministry are so effective. These flagship church resources reveal the proven ideas, programs, and principles that these churches have put into practice.

Flagship Church Resources currently available:

- *60 Simple Secrets Every Pastor Should Know*
- *The Perfectly Imperfect Church: Redefining the "Ideal Church"*
- *The Winning Spirit: Empowering Teenagers Through God's Grace*
- *Ultimate Skits: 20 Parables for Driving Home Your Point*
- *Doing Life With God: Real Stories Written by Students*
- *Doing Life With God 2: Real Stories Written by Students*
- *The Visual Edge: Compelling Video Connectors for Your Worship Experience*
- *Mission-Driven Worship: Helping Your Changing Church Celebrate God*
- *An Unstoppable Force: Daring to Become the Church God Had in Mind*
- *A Follower's Life: 12 Group Studies On What It Means to Walk With Jesus*

- *Leadership Essentials for Children's Ministry*
- *Keeping Your Head Above Water: Refreshing Insights for Church Leadership*
- *Seeing Beyond Church Walls: Action Plans for Touching Your Community*
- *unLearning Church: Just When You Thought You Had Leadership all Figured Out!*
- *Morph!: The Texture of Leadership for Tomorrow's Church*
- *The Quest for Christ: Discipling Today's Young Adults*
- *LeadingIdeas: To-the-Point Training for Christian Leaders*
- *Igniting Passion in Your Church: Becoming Intimate with Christ*
- *No More Lone Rangers: How to Build a Team-Centered Youth Ministry*

With more to follow!

No More Lone Rangers

HOW TO BUILD A
TEAM-CENTERED
YOUTH MINISTRY

By David Chow

Flagship church resources
from Group Publishing

No More Lone Rangers
HOW TO BUILD A TEAM-CENTERED YOUTH MINISTRY
Copyright © 2003 David Chow

Visit our Web site: **www.grouppublishing.com**

CREDITS
Editor: *Kelli B. Trujillo*
Creative Development Editor: *Amy Simpson*
Chief Creative Officer: *Joani Schultz*
Copy Editor: *Lyndsay E. Gerwing*
Book Designer: *Jean Bruns*
Print Production Artists: *Pat Miller and Joyce Douglas*
Cover Art Director/Designer: *Jeff A. Storm*
Production Manager: *Dodie Tipton*

LIBRARY OF CONGRESS CATALOGING-IN-PUBLICATION DATA
Chow, David.
No more lone rangers : how to build a team-centered youth ministry / by David Chow.
  p. cm.
  Includes bibliographical references.
  ISBN 0-7644-2419-X (pbk. : alk. paper)
  1. Church work with youth. I. Title.
  BV4447 .C477 2002
  259'.23--dc21   2002013279

10 9 8 7 6 5 4 3 2 1   12 11 10 09 08 07 06 05 04 03

Printed in the United States of America.

CONTENTS

dedication

This book is dedicated to my wife, Lori, who has supported me as a husband, father, pastor, and now as a writer. Your many hours of listening and editing have truly been God's gift to me.

This book is also dedicated to my mentor, Jim Burns. From the very beginning, you have encouraged me at every point in my ministry journey. Without your encouragement, this book may never have become a reality.

acknowledgments

I'd also like to say, "Thanks"...

to Group Publishing, and especially Kelli Trujillo, for all your support and encouragement as I learned the discipline and art of writing;

to Brian Manley, Terry Nyhuis, and Mike Shipman for your valuable feedback on my manuscript;

to my team members at the Crystal Cathedral who cheered me on and supported me as I wrote this book;

and to all the ministry team members I've had the privilege of serving with.

I'm thrilled for youth workers to read this book because I believe very strongly in a youth ministry having a healthy, adult, volunteer team. Actually, I believe it's impossible to have a strong youth ministry without volunteer leaders—"lone rangers" hurt the church. Lead youth workers must learn that youth ministry "success" is tied into their ability to find, train, encourage, and allow volunteers to do ministry with students.

I've watched many of my peers disappear from youth ministry because they ran their youth ministry as if their motto was "If it's to be, it's up to me." I think there would be a higher rate of youth ministry survival if the motto became something like "No more than four." One volunteer youth worker who cares for every four students—that would be great, and it would require a team.

Burnout, exhaustion, divorce, and contemplating suicide can be avoided when lead youth workers extend beyond their fears or ego and admit that they need help with students from within the church congregation. The lead youth worker who does everything for himself or herself limits the effectiveness of the ministry and literally takes away great ministry opportunities from adults within the church. Over my twenty-plus years as a youth pastor, I've found the greatest joys have been when adults recognize their gifts, discover a love for teenagers,

> *The lead youth worker who does everything for himself or herself limits the effectiveness of the ministry and literally takes away great ministry opportunities from adults within the church.*

and combine those to love students and point them to Jesus. Thankfully, I've been able to work myself out of ministry opportunities and responsibilities because I've learned the value of allowing and encouraging other adults to minister to students. I'm convinced that this is the major reason I've been able to last so long as a youth worker.

In this book, David has done a great job of defining some steps for building a leadership team. He has written with a nice balance between the why and how to. There's so much material in this book that it would be difficult to consume it all at once. Take your time reading this

By
Doug
Fields

book, and keep it close by your desk; read it, implement a few ideas, pull it out later, try something new, and read it again. You will want to continually refer to it as you develop and strengthen your leadership team. You may find yourself going back to the book just to reread some of the incredible quotes (the references he uses are worth the price of the book).

What I have appreciated about David over the years is that he's both a learner and a practitioner. He's always reading, attending seminars, thinking, asking questions, and trying new ideas within his ministry. He has written this book while also working in the church, so he's living out what he's writing about. (You can't write a book, survive, and keep a youth ministry going if you don't have a good team.)

You can do it; you just can't do it alone!

Doug Fields
Pastor to Students; Saddleback Church
www.dougfields.com

Are you getting tired? Do you feel like giving up? Are there more needs in your ministry than you're personally able to meet? *You're not alone.* Like you, youth workers across the country and around the world are struggling to meet the demands of ministry as they selflessly give their all to students. But, as you well know, sometimes giving our all isn't enough. Being a "lone ranger" in youth ministry just doesn't cut it.

Instead of doing all of the ministry yourself, bring others along with you to share the ministry! I'm not just talking about getting more "volunteers" to help set up chairs or to chaperone lock-ins. Hopefully by now, you've figured that out. What I'm talking about is intentionally putting together a *team of co-ministers*—people who will share in the inner workings of the ministry, not just "help" you do this or that.

Developing a team-centered youth ministry is both an exciting and challenging endeavor. It's exciting because there's nothing quite like being a part of a God-focused and God-honoring team. It's a powerful way to live out Jesus' teachings about unity and teamwork in ministry. But challenges come with the territory. Perhaps the most tremendous challenge is understanding that team-centered ministry doesn't just happen automatically. (If it did, we'd see a lot more ministries that are team-centered instead of person-centered!) This doesn't mean it's impossible, but that it *will* require dedication and hard work on your part. The good news is that as your ministry becomes

> **But, as you well know, sometimes giving our all isn't enough. Being a "lone ranger" in youth ministry just doesn't cut it.**

more team-centered, your load will be lightened, and you'll see more students' lives being changed.

While the main topic of *No More Lone Rangers* is leading a youth ministry team, at its heart this book is really about one basic goal: being effective and successful in youth ministry. Isn't that the goal for every youth worker? Doesn't every youth worker want to know that what he or she is doing is making a difference in the lives of students and families?

But what does it mean to be "successful" in youth ministry? Over the years, my own definition of success in youth ministry has changed dramatically. I've come to redefine success by the following six principles.

● Success is sharing ministry, not being a one-person show.

In my early years of ministry, I thought it was my job to do all the work while others cheered me on. However, as I spent more time in ministry, I realized I needed others. Not only was I getting tired, but there were certain aspects of youth ministry for which I just wasn't gifted. Having my own specific spiritual gifts and strengths, I needed others around me who were strong in areas where I was weak. Eventually I got tired of being a one-man show and taking a lone ranger approach to youth ministry, and I began to see involving others as a necessity instead of an option. Success for me was learning this lesson early on and inviting others to share in the joy of ministering to students and families.

● Success is modeling the body of Christ, not just teaching about it.

Teaching about teamwork simply requires comprehension; living it requires life transformation. Yet God is looking for churches and youth ministries that model the body of Christ in such a way that it is *undeniable* that they've been transformed by Jesus. Ultimately, my ministry with students will not be evaluated by what was taught, but by what was modeled. I'm not saying that we don't need solid teaching; what I am saying is that actions always speak louder than words.

● Success is caring for the students we have rather than worrying about the students we don't have.

Early on in youth ministry, I was more focused on reaching new students and increasing in numbers than caring for the students I already had. It wasn't until later that I realized God wouldn't bring me new students until I had adequately cared for the ones he'd already given me. In their book *The Youth Builder,* Jim Burns and Mike DeVries say it best: "We firmly believe that on the day we stand before God, He won't be asking us how many kids came to our ministries. He won't be delving into our programming. He'll want to know what we did with the students He entrusted to us. Are we faithful with the students He has entrusted to our care?"[1]

As I was faithful to care for the students God had given me, before I knew it, God started bringing new students for me to minister to.

● Success is more about what happens after students leave the youth ministry than what they do while they're in the ministry.

The question I always used to ask was "How many students are in the youth ministry?" What mattered to me back then was the number of students *currently* involved in the youth program. The question I should have asked instead was "Where will these students be ten years from now?" It wasn't until later that I realized that often when students graduate from the youth group, they also graduate from their faith.

Success in ministry is truly best measured by what happens in students' lives after they leave the youth ministry. If I catch up with students ten years after they've graduated and see that they're actively serving the Lord and faithfully living for him, then I've been successful. Like the parable of the sower (Matthew 13:1-23), I often don't get to see the results of my efforts until long after I've planted the seeds.

● Success should be viewed as a journey, not as a destination.

When I started out in ministry, I thought that with enough time and experience, "success" would eventually come. I'd reach a point at which everything was running smoothly, the ministry was continually growing and lives were being constantly changed.

The longer I'm in ministry, the more I realize that success is more of a process than a product. As much as I would like to believe that my ministry has "arrived," the reality is that I'm still growing and learning, just like everyone else. Writing this book has been a humbling experience because it has reminded me of the many areas in which our youth ministry needs to grow. Though I still keep focused on the ideal, I've

> *The longer I'm in ministry, the more I realize that success is more of a process than a product. As much as I would like to believe that my ministry has "arrived," the reality is that I'm still growing and learning, just like everyone else.*

had to realize that effective ministry is more of a journey than a destination. My job is to stay on the path and not get lost or sidetracked.

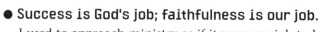

● Success is God's job; faithfulness is our job.

I used to approach ministry as if it were my job to be successful and God's job to be faithful to help me accomplish my goals. What I've realized, though, is that the equation needs to be reversed. It's *my* role to be faithful, and it's *God's* role to grant success. Everywhere I look in the Bible, I consistently see that it was God, not humans, who brought about success. God never commands us to be successful, but he does command us to be faithful to the things he has put us in charge of. In the parable of the talents (Matthew 25:14-30), Jesus teaches us that God rewards faithfulness, not success. The master doesn't say, "Well done, good and *successful* servant." Rather, he says, "Well done, good and *faithful* servant." When it comes down to it, success is more about what God does than what we do.

No More Lone Rangers is designed to help you become more successful and effective in your youth ministry by equipping you with specific strategies, tools, and ideas to build a team-centered youth ministry. Whether you're a lone ranger youth minister or you already have a team in place, *No More Lone Rangers* will help you discover ways you can magnify the impact your youth ministry has on the students in your church and community. This book will help you develop a clear vision for team-centered youth ministry and will point out ways to overcome the obstacles you'll encounter as you work to build up your team. You'll also find insight about recruiting team members, as well as suggestions for developing unity and understanding within the team. You'll get specific strategies for training and equipping team members for ministry, as well as lots of useful tips for helping team members take ownership of their parts in the ministry, moving from the mind-set of a volunteer to that of a co-minister.

Tools

At the end of each chapter in *No More Lone Rangers,* you'll find some helpful tools to assist you in processing and implementing what you've read.

• **Now What?**—These questions, evaluation tools, and ideas are designed to help you personally apply the principles you've just read about. They'll help you evaluate your own strengths and weaknesses, identify specific needs in your youth ministry, and implement suggestions to get you on your way to building up your team.

• **Team-Builder Questions**—A great way to use this book is to read it together as a team or to invite one or two key volunteers to read it with you. As you meet to discuss each chapter, these Team-Builder Questions will help you work as a group to process the information and dive deeper into the inner workings of your own ministry team.

Want to explore a particular topic? You'll also find a helpful **Recommended Reading** list at the end of the book. This short list highlights some other great resources about leadership, teamwork, and youth ministry. So if you're in a book-reading mood or you just can't stop thinking about team-centered youth ministry, flip to pages 140-142 for some of my reading suggestions.

So read on with anticipation and excitement. Most important, read with a desire to give God your best as you strive to develop a team-centered youth ministry.

ENDNOTES

1. *The Youth Builder* by Jim Burns, Ph.D., and Mike DeVries. Copyright © 2001. Regal Books, Ventura, CA 93003. Used by permission.

CHAPTER 1

The Vision for a Team-Centered Youth Ministry

"Had the church relied upon a single, incredibly gifted, magnetic individual to replace Jesus, the church would surely have collapsed. What the disciples discovered was that none of them had the complete package of gifts, abilities, and insights necessary to facilitate the growth of the Christian church, but each had a very significant and defined role to play in that revolutionary undertaking."

GEORGE BARNA, *THE POWER OF TEAM LEADERSHIP*[1]

One of my favorite movies is *Remember the Titans*, starring Denzel Washington and Will Patton. Based on real events and set during a time of racial strife, the movie depicts the heroic story of a football team composed of both black and white students who work together to win the state championship. Against all odds, Coach Herman Boone (played by Denzel Washington) helps the team members overcome their enormous differences and become a championship football team. The beauty of the movie is not that they won the state championship; it's what they accomplished through their commitment to unity and teamwork. Stories like these move us because they touch something deep inside that yearns for such an experience.

An even greater story of a team working together to overcome tremendous odds is the ministry team Jesus pulled together. He took a group of ordinary people with a wide range of backgrounds, personalities, and experience, and he built a team that impacted the world for him. The good news is that building and leading ministry teams that carry out God's purposes isn't limited to first-century Palestine or Jesus himself. I believe Jesus is inviting each of us to experience the excitement and energy that comes from leading a team of co-ministers. Our ability to impact students for Christ will be largely influenced by our ability to build and lead an effective ministry team.

Defining Team-Centered Youth Ministry

To understand what team-centered youth ministry looks like, one must start with a solid definition of what it is. I define team-centered youth ministry as "ministry with a diverse team of healthy, spiritually mature adults who share leadership and decision-making responsibilities, united by a vision to minister to young people and their families." Rather than youth ministry being left to the "professional youth worker," youth ministry becomes a shared calling. Everyone on the team contributes significantly to the success and effectiveness of the youth ministry. This team-centered approach to ministry can take place with a team of two or a team of two hundred.

> *Rather than youth ministry being left to the "professional youth worker," youth ministry becomes a shared calling.*

The Power of Team-Centered Youth Ministry

The real strength of a team-centered youth ministry lies in what it offers. The following are several important characteristics and benefits of taking a team-centered approach to youth ministry.

Team-Centered Ministry Models the Body of Christ in Action

Jesus taught his disciples: "Love one another. As I have loved you, so you must love one another. By this all men will know that you are my disciples, if you love one another" (John 13:34-35). In other words, the clearest evidence of being a Christian is the love we show to each other. When non-Christians see us loving one another, they can't help but take notice. They may not notice whether we smoke, swear, or drink, but they *will* notice when we love each other the way Christ loved us.

The same is true regarding the students in our youth ministries. When a youth ministry leadership team models Christian teamwork and love, students can't help but notice. When students see adult leaders praying, trusting, supporting, and forgiving each other, they see the body of Christ modeled to them in a powerful way. As Harold Westing wrote in the *Church Staff Handbook*, "If there is any place in the Christian world where people ought to be a genuine team, it is in the leadership of the church...The staff must be a microcosm of the body of Christ, a church in miniature."[2]

We can talk to our students all day about being the body of Christ, but if our team isn't modeling it, it will never happen in the youth group. One of the most powerful benefits of a team-centered youth ministry is the example it sets for students. I experienced this firsthand when I was a college student. It was clear to me that the college ministry staff loved each other and enjoyed working as a team. Whether it was through their humorous skits, public appreciation of each other, or obvious team unity, they were modeling the body of Christ in action. Their love for each other had a significant impact on our college group. We began to display what we had seen modeled by the leadership team. Likewise, if you begin modeling the body of Christ as a team, before you know it, you'll see the same love and teamwork shining forth in your students' lives.

Team-Centered Ministry Is Relevant to a Postmodern World

Remember the old *Star Trek* series? Created in the mid-'60s, *Star Trek* starred William Shatner as Captain Kirk, the leader of a crew of intergalactic travelers. Captain Kirk was a highly independent, emotional, and aggressive leader. He regularly made unilateral decisions, constantly broke the "prime directive" to not interfere with other planets' affairs. Over the years, though, the leadership style depicted in *Star Trek* evolved. About two decades after the first *Star Trek* show premiered, *Star Trek: The Next Generation* hit the airwaves, starring Patrick Stewart as Captain Picard. In *The Next Generation*, Captain Picard had quite a different leadership style from Captain Kirk; Picard was a team-oriented, diplomatic, and compassionate leader. Sharing leadership with others, following the prime directive, and drawing upon the wisdom of others were common themes in *The Next Generation*. The contrast between Kirk and Picard illustrates more than just a change of scriptwriters; it represents a cultural shift from an older model of leadership to a newer one. It corresponds to a transition from modernism to postmodernism.

This newer postmodern approach to leadership can be seen not just in the world of interplanetary exploration, but also in the church. Youth ministry today is a lot different from youth ministry twenty or thirty years ago. In the past, youth ministry was seen as an individual sport rather than a team sport. The old model was one leader and many followers; today's model is many leaders and fewer followers. The old style of leadership was a top-down approach with decision-making limited to

The old model was one leader and many followers; today's model is many leaders and fewer followers.

a few; today's style is a team-centered approach with decision-making shared by many. The old model used *I*. Today's model uses *we*.

While it may be easier for us to stick with the older, more established model of leadership, our ministry effectiveness will be limited. Team-centered youth ministry is the most relevant model to today's culture and the students we are trying to reach. If we want to be relevant to our postmodern culture, then we need to move toward a team-centered youth ministry.

Working With a Team Multiplies the Level of Ministry

According to *Webster's New World College Dictionary*, the law of synergism is defined as "the simultaneous action of separate agencies which, together, have greater total effect than the sum of their individual effects." In other words, the results of various forces working together will be greater than all the individual parts added together. You can clearly see synergism at work in a team-centered youth ministry. When teams are functioning at their best, ministry multiplies far beyond what each team member could do on his or her own. Behind every great ministry is a great group of co-ministers. The point person may get the most press, but if you look a little deeper, you'll find a well-oiled, high-functioning team.

Ministry just isn't the same without a team. It's amazing the difference teams make to a ministry. For example:

• Effective teams extend the ministry well beyond a single person. Instead of only having one "minister," teams create many "ministers."

• Effective teams raise the quality of ministry programs and events to a higher level. Rather than ministry being limited by the creativity and ability of one or a few individuals, teams bring a synergistic force to the planning, preparing, and implementing of youth programs. Great ideas are discovered, ownership is shared, and the quality of ministry is enhanced.

• Effective teams expand the number and types of students being ministered to. Certain students relate better to certain adults. *No one* can relate effectively to every student. A diverse team of adults opens the door for a youth ministry to reach a larger number and variety of students. Growing your team contributes to growing your youth ministry.

At my current ministry, I was reminded of this truth in a powerful way. Shortly after joining the staff at the Crystal Cathedral, the entire youth staff transitioned to other ministries for various reasons. This included volunteers, interns, and paid staff. Having come from a church where I had developed a highly functioning team, I immediately noticed the drop in ministry quality. I could only minister to so many students, and my programs were limited to my personal creativity and energy. It was a breath of fresh air when I finally got a team in place. Even the students in the ministry noticed the difference. Several teenagers told me that they liked youth group bet-

> *I could only minister to so many students, and my programs were limited to my personal creativity and energy. It was a breath of fresh air when I finally got a team in place.*

ter now that I had a team of people helping out. (I'm glad I didn't take it personally!)

Team-Centered Ministry Minimizes the Weaknesses of Others

The beauty of a team-centered youth ministry is that it minimizes the weaknesses of others because it focuses on people's strengths. Weaknesses are kept to a minimum when everyone on the team is serving in his or her area of giftedness. Unlike a program-centered ministry in which volunteers are used to fill in open "slots" and are stuck wherever there is a need, in team-centered ministry, leaders minister based on their strengths.

This is a basic principle in competitive sports. A coach's job is to help athletes find and develop their strengths. If sprinting is an athlete's strength, then a good coach will help him or her identify this strength and will have the athlete compete in sprints. Putting a sprinter in a long-distance event is not only bad coaching, but it also can create intense frustration and dissatisfaction for the athlete. I learned this lesson myself in high school. As a competitive swimmer, I discovered that I was best at short-distance events such as the 50-yard or 100-yard sprint. I loved swimming fast, and I was good at it. I felt a sense of satisfaction because I saw my hard work yield success. But if my coach had put me in the 500-yard freestyle, the stands would've been emptied as everybody went home—because it would have taken me *forever* to finish the event. My coach understood that for our team to win, he needed to place us where we were strongest, thus minimizing our weaknesses and maximizing our strengths.

The same is true for ministry. When team members are serving where they are strongest, everyone benefits. One of my youth worker friends struggles with leading games. Whenever he leads games, they lack energy and creativity. When he begins work at a new church, one of the first things he does is find someone who enjoys leading games and is good at it. Once he finds the right person, his own weakness becomes a non-issue.

The opposite is true with his strengths. While my friend isn't that great at leading games, he is gifted in the area of teaching. He enjoys it and students gain a lot from his lessons. The more he is able to focus on teaching, the more the youth ministry benefits. The strength of a team-centered approach comes into play when team members begin to serve where they are strongest instead of where they are weakest.

Teamwork Promotes Excitement and Energy

Excitement and energy are natural results of being part of a healthy and strong team. Ministry is more fun when you're working side by side with others. There is a unique joy found in celebrating experiences together (such as a student turning his life over to Christ). When you're on a team, excitement is contagious and momentum develops.

Not only does being part of a team create excitement, but it also provides the energy necessary to accomplish great tasks. No significant task in history was ever accomplished alone. Great accomplishments are *always* a team effort. When reading the book of Acts, one doesn't have to look far to see the incredible things God accomplished through a committed team of Christians. Just look at the way teamwork and ministry worked hand in hand for the early Christians: "All the believers were together and had everything in common. Selling their possessions and goods, they gave to anyone as he had need. Every day they continued to meet together in the temple courts. They broke bread in their homes and ate together with glad and sincere hearts, praising God and enjoying the favor of all the people. And the Lord added to their number daily those who were being saved" (Acts 2:44-47).

Another advantage of working with a team is that it can provide you with the strength to overcome great challenges. Every ministry faces tremendous challenges at one time or another—a student dies, a family experiences divorce, a car accident occurs during a youth trip, attendance dramatically declines, or a key student leader renounces her faith. Rather than facing the challenge alone, a team can come alongside you and face the challenge together. One challenge every youth worker faces is burnout. Without a team to encourage and energize you, burnout is not far away. Many youth workers have learned this lesson the hard way at the expense of their physical, emotional, and spiritual health. Rather than a youth minister having to spin too many plates, a ministry team can help share the load of ministry.

Team-Centered Ministry Produces New Leaders

In his book *Unsung Heroes,* youth ministry veteran Les Christie points out what should be a primary goal of youth workers, saying, "Most youth workers are drawn to youth ministry by their love for young people and desire to serve. But a primary task of the youth worker is also to develop other adults who will in turn work with young people. The long-term effectiveness of youth ministry depends on the ability of the youth worker to develop a team of committed adult volunteers."[3] Ministries that follow the person-centered model of leadership produce *followers.* When all the direction and control comes from one person, team members learn and practice following rather than leading. Instead of being released and empowered for ministry, they become dependent on the youth leader for guidance and supervision. Even though a person-centered ministry may be able to develop a strong youth ministry program, it will never develop strong leaders.

Ministries that are team-centered produce leaders. When people are on a team, everyone has a role that becomes vital to the success of the ministry. As team members take ownership of their roles, they naturally develop their leadership abilities. Instead of just cranking out more followers, a team-centered youth ministry expands the leadership base, and a stronger ministry is the inevitable result of developing strong leaders.

Even though a person-centered ministry may be able to develop a strong youth ministry program, it will never develop strong leaders.

Jesus' investment in his disciples is a perfect model of multiplying leadership. Jesus knew that his time on earth was limited, and he made it a priority to develop his disciples into leaders who would carry on the mission to "go and make disciples" after he was no longer physically with them. Jesus multiplied his ministry by developing leaders who would, in turn, reach the world.

Is your primary goal to develop a strong youth program? Or is it to develop strong youth leaders who will go out and impact students and families for Christ? One of the goals of team-centered youth ministry is to produce new leaders. The more leaders your ministry produces, the more ministry you'll be able to accomplish.

A Team Approach Benefits the Ministry Long Term

Too often we focus on the short term when it comes to building a youth ministry. We worry about how many kids are coming to youth group tonight; rarely do we really think about what shape the ministry would be in if we were no longer around due to a move, career change, or other circumstance. I've seen it time and time again: A youth worker builds a ministry around himself or herself, only to see it completely crumble after he or she leaves. Believe it or not, I've even met youth workers who felt this was a sign of good leadership!

If you build a ministry around yourself and your personality, then it's likely that when you leave, so will your ministry. But if you build a ministry around a team, the ministry will continue on even if you leave.

This really hit home for me a few years ago. After attending a funeral at a church I had served at previously, the church's associate pastor (whom I'd never met) encouraged me by sharing that the team I had put into place years ago was still serving faithfully in the youth ministry. Even though they had experienced several youth pastors since my departure, the team became an anchoring point for the youth ministry. From that point on, I realized that building a team benefits the ministry not just for the short term, but more importantly for the long term. I think that's what Jesus had in mind from the very beginning when he recruited, developed, and empowered his team of disciples.

CHARACTERISTICS OF A TEAM-CENTERED YOUTH MINISTRY

A team-centered approach to youth ministry will…
• model the body of Christ in action,
• be relevant to a postmodern world,
• multiply the level of ministry,
• minimize people's weaknesses,
• promote excitement and energy,
• produce new leaders, and
• benefit the ministry long term.

Conclusion

Hopefully by now you're convinced of the value and importance of a team-centered youth ministry. In the chapters that follow, you'll learn how to overcome some obstacles of developing a team-centered youth ministry, and more importantly, you'll learn how to recruit, inspire, understand, care for, connect, train, and release teams for ministry.

Now What?

Take a moment to evaluate the following areas of your youth ministry by checking the box for every "yes" answer. When you've finished, total up your score, but don't be too hard on yourself if you don't score as well you would've liked to. Use this evaluation tool to help you identify areas you'd like to focus on as you read this book.

PERSONAL BALANCE INVENTORY

❑ YES Do you consistently ask others to help you instead of taking on responsibilities and tasks on your own?

❑ YES Do you rarely experience moments of "burnout" or "ministry fatigue"?

❑ YES Do you regularly feel joy and enthusiasm for ministry?

❑ YES Do you set strict boundaries that do not allow ministry time to interfere with time for family and friends?

❑ YES Is the success of the ministry dependent upon several people instead of being limited only to what you can do personally?

Healthy Balance—4 to 5 checked boxes
Average Balance—2 to 3 checked boxes
Unhealthy Balance—0 to 1 checked boxes

LEADERSHIP BASE INVENTORY

❑ YES Are your current volunteers developing their leadership abilities?

❑ YES Do you have regular, ongoing training for youth leaders?

❑ YES Do you share decision-making responsibilities with your leaders?

❑ YES Are you surrounding yourself with leaders who are strong where you are weak?

❑ YES If you were to leave tomorrow, would the ministry be able to continue successfully without your presence?

Multiplying Leaders—4 to 5 checked boxes
Working on Empowering Leaders—2 to 3 checked boxes
Lone Ranger Ministry—0 to 1 checked boxes

TEAM MORALE INVENTORY

❑ YES   Is there energy and excitement within your leadership team?

❑ YES   Does your leadership team love one another as "Christ loved us"?

❑ YES   Are your leaders serving in their areas of strength and gifted-ness?

❑ YES   Does the leadership team "come together" under crisis and challenge?

❑ YES   Do your leaders display "ownership" of the youth ministry?

High Morale—4 to 5 checked boxes

Average Morale—2 to 3 checked boxes

Low Morale—0 to 1 checked boxes

Team-Builder Questions

These questions are to help facilitate discussion for teams reading this book together. Feel free to add additional questions or use the ones that work best for the team.

1. What makes working together as a healthy team so appealing?

2. Which characteristics of a team-centered youth ministry excite you the most?

3. Which characteristic is most clearly seen on the team? Which characteristic does the team need to work on the most?

4. What things can we do as a team to better model the body of Christ to our students?

5. What are ways we can minimize our personal weaknesses through sharing our strengths?

6. What things are we doing as a team that benefit the ministry long term?

ENDNOTES

1. Reprinted from *The Power of Team Leadership*, Copyright © 2001 by George Barna. Used by permission of WaterBrook Press, Colorado Springs, CO. All rights reserved.
2. Taken from *Church Staff Handbook* © 1985, 1997 by Harold J. Westing. Published by Kregel Publications, Grand Rapids, MI. Used by permission. All rights reserved.
3. Taken from *Unsung Heroes* by Les Christie. Copyright © 1987 by Youth Specialties, Inc. Used by permission of Zondervan.

CHAPTER 2

Overcoming Obstacles

"We would be surprised how much can be accomplished when we don't care who gets the credit!"

WAYNE CORDEIRO,

DOING CHURCH AS A TEAM[1]

Although I played sports most of my life, I had a hard time staying in shape once I graduated from college. While everything I'd read and heard told me to exercise regularly, I found it a real struggle to actually *do* it. As a result, I started to gain weight. It got so bad that one Christmas my brother told me, "It's good to see you again—every year I get to see *more* of you!"

After that, I decided it was time to do something about it. The problem was, every time I set out to lose weight (and I tried several times), I failed. Even though I had several books on exercising and staying healthy, I just couldn't put into practice what I knew. What I had failed to do was properly identify and overcome the specific obstacles preventing me from getting into shape. I hadn't really factored in issues in my life such as busyness, poor eating habits, expecting immediate results, and giving up after setbacks. It wasn't until I took these obstacles seriously that I was able to successfully accomplish my goals.

In a similar way, youth workers setting out to develop a team-centered youth ministry will face many obstacles. Identifying and understanding these obstacles, and working to overcome them, will be a critical step toward developing a successful team-centered youth ministry.

Obstacles to Team-Centered Youth Ministry

While all youth workers face challenges that are unique to their ministries and leadership styles, the following pages explain the most common obstacles you'll face when you set out to develop a team-centered youth ministry.

Inexperience

It's difficult to know how to lead a team-centered youth ministry if you've never done it before. Very few youth workers in ministry today got to see a team-centered approach modeled for them while they were preparing for ministry. In most cases, the leadership style they saw modeled was person-centered instead of team-centered. This lack of exposure and experience can prevent youth workers from even beginning the journey to team-centered ministry. In general, we tend to avoid what we don't know how to do.

While feeling inadequate and unprepared may seem like an insurmountable obstacle, it can also be a powerful catalyst that causes us to fully depend on God. 2 Corinthians 12:9a reminds us of an important truth when God tells Paul, "My grace is sufficient for you, for my power is made perfect in weakness." It's not our *ability* that God cares about but our *availability* to his purposes. If God is calling us to develop a team-centered youth ministry, he will provide the needed strength and resources to accomplish this task.

> *It's not our **ability** that God cares about but our **availability** to his purposes. If God is calling us to develop a team-centered youth ministry, he will provide the needed strength and resources to accomplish this task.*

Another thing to keep in mind is that learning is a lifelong task for every leader. If there is one critical thing I've learned in ministry, it's that the longer I'm in ministry, the more I need to increase instead of decrease my learning. I remember sitting at a large youth ministry convention and hearing Howard Hendricks say some powerful words that are true for all of us who work with students: "The minute you stop learning is the minute you stop leading." Rather than allowing inexperience to be an excuse for not learning, inexperience can, instead, motivate us to learn new skills or abilities.

As a result, I've learned to love failure. Experimenting, trying new things, and making discoveries along the way have become normal parts of ministry for me. Failure can be a great teacher. As I look back over my work with students, it becomes clear that I've learned more from failure than I have from success. So if inexperience is an obstacle blocking your path, take time to learn from other youth workers who are leading team-centered youth ministries. Don't be afraid to ask for help and allow God to work powerfully in your weakness.

Negative Past Experiences

An obstacle just as intimidating as inexperience is past negative experience. Many youth workers have only seen negative or unhealthy examples of "teamwork" in youth ministry. Instead of seeing a loving team in action, they've seen teams who don't like each other, who stab each other in the back, who have separate agendas, or who don't trust each other.

At one of the churches I served, I experienced firsthand the difficulties of working in an unhealthy and dysfunctional team. Outside of the formal working environment, team members didn't get along, talked behind each other's backs, disagreed on fundamental issues, and viewed their own parts of the ministry as competing with each other. It was a discouraging environment to work in, to say the least. What I learned from that experience is that healthy, high-functioning teams are the exception, not the rule. It's more natural for teams to allow pride, competitiveness, and selfishness to influence them than humility, teamwork, and servanthood. As a result, great teams don't happen by accident; they require hard work, patience, and dependence on God.

Take comfort in the fact that even Jesus had negative experiences working with his team of disciples. Remember when James and John asked Jesus whether they could have their own special rights and privileges (Matthew 20:20-23)? Or how about all the times in the gospels when we see Peter acting impulsively and independently from the rest of the group (Matthew 14:28; 16:22; John 18:10)? Let's not forget the negative impact Judas had in the group for the entire three years he spent with Jesus (Mark 14:10, John 12:4-6). Yet despite the negative experiences Jesus had with his disciples, he persevered to the end and trusted that the Holy Spirit would finish what he started. The book of Acts contains the wonderful story of how God used Jesus' "team" to turn the world upside down for Christ.

If you've been burned by past experiences that were poor examples of "teamwork," don't allow those negative experiences to control your future. Learn from them, but don't allow them to hinder you from developing a team-centered youth ministry. Turn your negative experiences into positive ones by applying what you've learned to your current ministry.

The Need to Be in Control

The most common obstacle to a team-centered youth ministry is the desire to be in control. When we need to have ministry done "our way," when we need to be involved in every ministry decision, and when we refuse others the freedom to fail, we have a control issue. Hans Finzel explains it this way in *Empowered Leaders*: "A control freak thinks he has all the answers, thinks he knows best because he was there first, has 'founder-itis' (is unable to let go of what he started), delegates responsibilities but no authority to go with them, loves to control by keeping people in the dark, reverses decisions others have made, and doesn't give others room to make their own mark."[2]

The most common reason we feel the need to control is our own insecurity. Often this insecurity stems from a fear that if we give others power and influence, they'll hurt us and the ministry. Yet, even though Jesus knew that Judas would betray him, he took the risk of granting him control and influence along with the other disciples. Judas was even put in charge of the group's finances (John 13:29). Instead of allowing insecurity to control him, Jesus allowed his confidence in God's plan to dictate his actions and decisions.

The most common reason we feel the need to control is our own insecurity.

We're often motivated to cling tightly to control because we fear that if others are successful and look good, then we look bad. We feel like we need to be the superstar or the only one in the limelight. Sometimes we worry that if others do well, then maybe the church won't need us anymore. When feelings like this arise, we need to remind ourselves that our role is to prepare and equip people for ministry (Ephesians 4:11-13). When team members are doing what God is calling them to do, not only are they successful in God's eyes, but so are you.

Another cause of the drive to control is fearing failure to the point that we won't allow anyone to take chances and learn from their own trials and errors. Instead, we go around fixing everything they've done or coming to the rescue when something goes wrong. Releasing control may result in some failures, but the greater failure is not trusting God enough to let him teach others through their own efforts and mistakes.

In my life, my need to control has only hindered, not helped, the youth ministry. One example is a time I asked an adult leader to plan our annual winter retreat. He did a great job of finding a cabin, registering the kids, securing transportation, and planning the program. The only problem was that once we got to the cabin, I took over. Instead of working behind the scenes and supporting him, I instinctively took control and wasted a perfect opportunity to help him develop as a leader. Not only did my behavior hurt his feelings, but it also communicated that I always had to be in control.

Until we learn to loosen our own controlling grip on our youth ministries and trust God to work through others too, we will never achieve the unity and effectiveness God desires for a team-centered ministry. After all, imagine what the fate of the church would have been if Jesus hadn't released control to his disciples and developed them as leaders!

The Desire for Efficiency

Another common obstacle to a team-centered youth ministry is the desire for efficiency. As you may have already experienced, there are definite advantages to doing ministry alone. For example:

• Ministry gets done faster. If you want something done; you simply go out and do it. You don't have to coordinate or work with anyone except yourself.

• Ministry is more predictable and controllable. Because people are unpredictable, removing others from the process means that you have complete control of the task.

• You get all the credit when ministry goes well. When you're the only one doing ministry, then you'll get all the kudos for a job well done.

There is no question that doing ministry alone is more efficient than doing ministry as a team. The problem is that the drawbacks of this approach far outweigh the advantages. For example, when doing ministry alone:

• Ministries lose momentum and lack depth. There is only so much one person can do. While it's easier to start things by yourself, you'll have difficulty maintaining momentum. Ministering to students without developing leaders results in a shallow, program-focused youth ministry. Your programs may be a mile wide but an inch deep.

• Fewer people are ministered to. There are only so many students you can effectively minister to when you're doing ministry alone. Regardless of how much energy you have, there will always be a limit to how many students you can personally care for. Even if your youth group is very small, you'll at least need someone of the opposite sex to minister to the other "half" of the youth group.

• Team members become spectators. When we do ministry alone, we communicate to others that their role is to watch ministry, not do ministry. Instead of preparing God's people for ministry, we are preparing them to be consumers and spectators.

> *When we do ministry alone, we communicate to others that their role is to watch ministry, not do ministry. Instead of preparing God's people for ministry, we are preparing them to be consumers and spectators.*

• You get all the blame when things don't go well. I'm not suggesting that you shouldn't receive a part of the blame when troubles arise, but when you're doing ministry alone, you shoulder *all* the blame.

• The greatest risk to doing ministry alone is personal and ministry burnout. Doing ministry alone is like trying to spin as many plates as possible. There are only so many plates you can spin before they all come crashing down. All of us can feel burned out and in need of rest and renewal, but doing ministry alone can cause you to burn out to the point that you're no good to your family, your students, or your church.

Character Issues

Often an obstacle to developing a team-centered youth ministry is the leader himself or herself. While the problem may be an issue of competence, it's more often an issue of character. In the end, *who we are* as leaders is more important than what we *do* as leaders. Developing a team-centered youth ministry will be hindered if we lack character as a Christian leader.

The problem is that we're often so focused on the competence side of leadership that we neglect the character side of leadership. While both are important, when a leader fails to develop and maintain a Christlike character, his or her ability to lead others will be hindered. God works *in* a leader before he works *through* a leader, so it's critical that a leader keep both competence and character in balance.

Being a person of character means living with integrity. A person of integrity is someone who is the same on the inside and outside. There are not two sides to the person. The leader may not be perfect, but he or she is honest and trustworthy. Being people of integrity means that we keep our word. If we say we'll do something or be somewhere at a certain time, we do it. Wayne Cordeiro described it this way in his book *Doing Church as a Team*: "Character is the ability to follow through on a worthy decision long after the emotion of making that decision has passed."[3] Being a person of integrity leaves no room for inconsistencies and contradictions. If teammates see that we lack integrity, they will not trust or follow us.

Being a person of character also means having a servant attitude toward others. In the secular world, leaders are elevated above those that follow them. Leaders often use their power to coerce and manipulate those "below" them. Jesus, who recognized the disciples' struggle with this, shared the following: "You know that the rulers of the Gentiles lord it over them, and their high officials exercise authority over them. Not so with you. Instead, whoever wants to become great among you must be your servant, and whoever wants to be first must be your slave—just as the Son of Man did not come to be served, but to serve, and to give his life as a ransom for many" (Matthew 20:25-28).

Jesus wanted his disciples to understand that Christian leadership is not about pride, but humility; it's not about getting, but giving; it's not about being served, but serving others. One of the true marks of a Christian leader is that person's desire and commitment to serve others.

An Inability to Keep Volunteers

Sometimes the obstacle to a team-centered youth ministry is not how to recruit team members, but how to keep team members from leaving. There are a variety of reasons team members can begin to feel so discouraged that they want to quit. Kenneth Gangel, in *Feeding & Leading*, identifies ten reasons volunteers leave the ministry. Take a look at the list, and see if you can identify issues with which your own teammates or volunteers may be dealing.

1. Volunteers become overworked and burned out.

2. Volunteers don't receive much-needed help.

3. Volunteers have personal and spiritual needs that aren't being met in the framework of their ministries.

4. Volunteers are not adequately shown appreciation.

5. Volunteers have not been provided proper equipment and materials.

6. Volunteers have not been trained adequately for the ministries they have been asked to carry out.

7. Volunteers have developed friction between or among workers in

a given ministry area.

8. Volunteers have lost interest, enthusiasm, and commitment for ministry.

9. Volunteers experience supervision that is inadequate or abrasive.

10. Volunteer evaluations have not been carried out or results have not been identified as a positive thrust for ministry improvement.[4]

Caring for volunteers is delicate work because mistreating volunteers is easy to do. When you proactively work to keep volunteers from leaving the ministry, you'll be on your way to developing a team-centered youth ministry.

Conclusion

Facing obstacles is a normal and natural part of developing a team-centered youth ministry. Change, no matter how positive or beneficial, is always a difficult process. Change brings insecurity, insecurity leads to fear, and fear results in resistance. The early church experienced tremendous obstacles; persecution, discouragement, and even death were common experiences for those first Christians. Despite the many obstacles they experienced, with God's power, the early church learned to overcome them. Paul reminds us of this truth when he says: "We are hard pressed on every side, but not crushed; perplexed, but not in despair; persecuted, but not abandoned; struck down, but not destroyed. We always carry around in our body the death of Jesus, so that the life of Jesus may also be revealed in our body" (2 Corinthians 4:8-10).

Change, no matter how positive or beneficial, is always a difficult process. Change brings insecurity, insecurity leads to fear, and fear results in resistance.

Don't let obstacles cause you to give up on your pursuit of developing a team-centered youth ministry. Learn to see obstacles not as permanent problems but as temporary challenges. Ministry challenges are always great opportunities for growth. It's through these challenges that God strengthens our dependence on him and helps us grow in faith. Just remember: Before change can be embraced by others, it must start with the determination in the heart of the leader. If the leader isn't willing to face the challenges of change, then those who follow won't be either.

NOW WHAT?

1. Share with a friend which of the obstacles mentioned in this chapter you struggle with most.

2. Identify a ministry and leader you know about that positively model a team-centered approach.

3. What are three specific ways you can begin releasing control of your ministry to other leaders?

4. Ask someone close to you to identify potential character flaws in you as a leader.

5. In what ways have you struggled to keep volunteers? How can you prevent it from happening in the future?

Team-Builder Questions

1. Why is failing to identify obstacles detrimental to us achieving our goals?

2. Which of the obstacles in this chapter do you most identify with and why?

3. What are ways one can overcome the obstacle of needing to control ministry?

4. If doing ministry alone seems more efficient, why is it not worth it in the long run?

5. What are areas in your personal leadership style and ability that might hinder developing a team-centered youth ministry?

6. How can we avoid losing volunteers based on our past experiences?

ENDNOTES

1. *Doing Church as a Team* by Wayne Cordeiro. Copyright © 2001. Regal Books, Ventura, CA 93003. Used by permission.
2. *Empowered Leaders*, Hans Finzel, © 1998, W Publishing Group, Nashville, Tennessee. All rights reserved.
3. *Doing Church as a Team* by Wayne Cordeiro. Copyright © 2001. Regal Books, Ventura, CA 93003. Used by permission.
4. Adapted from *Feeding & Leading*, copyright © 1989 Kenneth O. Gangel. Used by permission of Baker Books, a Division of Baker Book House Company.

CHAPTER 3

Recruiting Your Team

"Recruitment of volunteers is perhaps the most unglamorous part of youth ministry, even though it's one of the most essential. Besides being unglamorous, recruitment can be difficult; not all adults readily respond to the challenge of working with young people— but, then again, not all adults should."
LES CHRISTIE, *UNSUNG HEROES*[1]

It was my first discipleship group, and I was really looking forward to the opportunity to help students grow spiritually. The only problem was that when I advertised it to the youth group, I told everyone to come. As a result, several students who weren't interested in growing spiritually showed up. Instead of helping students grow spiritually, I ended up spending most of my time disciplining them and passing out Ritalin (just kidding)! It became such a problem that I ended up canceling the group after about a month and a half. Looking back at the experience, I realize that if I would have been more clear about the purpose of the group and recruited only the students who wanted to grow spiritually, I could have avoided many of those problems.

While recruiting students for a discipleship group may not be your greatest challenge, recruiting quality youth leaders probably will be. Top-notch youth leaders are hard to find no matter what church you serve in or how long you've been in ministry. The good news is that you're not alone. Recruiting Christlike, capable leaders has *never* been easy. Even in the Old Testament, God himself had a hard time finding a spiritual leader for Israel: "I looked for someone who might rebuild the wall of righteousness that guards the land. I searched for someone to stand in the gap in the wall so I wouldn't have to destroy the land, but I found no one" (Ezekiel 22:30, New Living Translation). Jesus also recognized the scarcity of quality leaders when he told his disciples, "The harvest is plentiful but the workers are few" (Matthew 9:37).

Struggling to find leaders to help minister to students will be a never-ending task for every youth worker. In every ministry I've ever served, I've struggled to find leaders. While there were times it came easily, most of the time it required continual prayer and persistence. There were many times when I felt like giving up out of sheer frustration. But I had to remind myself that giving up and failing to recruit more leaders was not an option if I truly wanted to develop a team-centered youth ministry.

Who to Recruit

Before actually recruiting potential leaders, it's important to think through who you are trying to recruit. Not everyone is called to work with youth, nor *should* everyone work with youth. Depending on a person's gifts, personality, and experiences, youth ministry may or may not be where God is calling them to serve. When it comes down to it, knowing who to recruit is more critical than knowing how to recruit. If we miss this point, we may be tempted to recruit the next warm body that walks through our youth room door.

When it comes down to it, knowing who to recruit is more critical than knowing how to recruit. If we miss this point, we may be tempted to recruit the next warm body that walks through our youth room door.

Because recruiting leaders is always easier than asking them to leave, you'll inevitably pay a price if you recruit the wrong type of person. When it comes to recruiting youth leaders, quality is always more important than quantity. Part of the reason for this is that your current leaders will attract and set the tone for the future leaders.

I experienced this firsthand at a previous church. When I arrived at the church, I inherited a longtime volunteer. He had a great heart and had been faithful to the youth ministry. The only problem was that he saw his role more as that of a chaperone than as a minister to students. As I recruited new leaders, they followed his example and chose to relate to students as chaperones. It wasn't until I recruited another leader who had previous youth ministry experience that the pattern was broken. Because of her commitment to investing in students, she became an example for the other leaders. Not only did her ministry heart influence the existing leaders, but it also set the tone for the future leaders. The moral of the story: Don't settle for just anyone—recruit only the *right* type of leaders.

When recruiting leaders, look for people with the following qualities.

A Genuine Relationship With Christ

You want leaders who love Christ first and foremost. Before worrying about whether they love students, worry about whether they love Christ with all their heart, soul, mind, and strength. Because you're in the business of influencing students spiritually, it's critical that your leaders exemplify a sincere love for Christ. Leaders will never be able to take students farther than they are spiritually. Discovering how a potential leader made a faith commitment to Christ, what the spiritually defining moments in his or her life have been, and what actions the person takes to keep growing spiritually are essential to learning about that potential leader's relationship with Christ.

A Positive Christian Witness

In tandem to a person's relationship with Christ is a possible leader's Christian witness. Students may not always follow what we say, but they will always follow what we do. It must be obvious to others that our leaders' love for Christ is demonstrated by their words and actions. While you're not looking for perfect leaders, you are looking for leaders who are committed to living "above reproach" (1 Timothy 3:2). Leaders with a positive Christian witness demonstrate Christlike character, steer clear of sin and temptation, place Christ first in all areas of their lives, and are prayerfully dependent on the Holy Spirit. One of my friends calls it a "No Doubt" lifestyle: There is no doubt that this person loves Christ with all his or her heart.

> **IMPORTANT QUALITIES IN POTENTIAL YOUTH LEADERS:**
> - The person has a genuine relationship with Christ.
> - His or her lifestyle is a positive Christian witness.
> - The person has a calling to work with youth.
> - He or she is committed to the larger church.
> - The person is a team player.

A Calling to Work With Youth

Youth ministry is more of a calling than it is a career. What sane person would choose to work with rambunctious, emotionally driven, and inconsistent teenagers for little or no pay? Working with students is truly a calling from God. You can tell when a person doesn't have a calling because teenagers generally get on his or her nerves.

Having a calling to work with youth is more than just being able to relate to adolescents. It's having a deep passion to come alongside students and help them walk with Christ. It's our calling that gives us the power to keep loving students in spite of their shortcomings and failures. It's our calling that gives us the courage to enter into the world of young people despite our fear and discomfort. It's our calling that empowers us to remain faithful to students even after they become unfaithful to us. Recruit people who sense this calling. They may not be able to articulate it as such, but you can't miss it when you see it.

Commitment to the Larger Church

Having a commitment to the larger church is just as vital as having a call to work with teenagers. Youth ministry exists to support the larger church, not to replace it. Youth leaders need to view themselves and their ministry as working to build up the entire church body, not just the youth ministry. Youth leaders must fully support the values and goals of the larger church, as well as the church leadership God has put in place. Faithful attendance to the main church service as well as agreement with the mission and philosophy of the church's ministry is essential. If a person is new to the church and is interested in helping with the youth ministry, I recommend asking that person to attend the church for at least six months before considering becoming a youth leader. Recruiting leaders who are not committed to the larger church is a dangerous practice and only discourages students from successfully transitioning into the larger church. If your youth leaders don't love the church, how will your students ever come to love it?

> **If your youth leaders don't love the church, how will your students ever come to love it?**

A Team Player

If your goal is to develop a team-centered youth ministry, you'll want to recruit team players—leaders who understand the concept of teamwork. They understand that they need others and that God has designed the church family to work with each other, not against each other. Paul speaks about this in his letter to the Corinthians, saying, "The body is a unit, though it is made up of many parts; and though all its parts are many, they form one body. So it is with Christ...God has arranged the parts in the body, every one of them, just as he wanted them to be...If one part suffers, every part suffers with it; if one part is honored, every part rejoices with it. Now you are the body of Christ, and each one of you is a part of it" (1 Corinthians 12:12, 18, 26-27).

Team players are committed to the success of the team and to each other. Team players practice open and honest communication and willingly work through conflicts quickly and appropriately (Matthew 5:23-24). And finally, team players are willing to own up to their mistakes and learn from each other. Your team is only as strong as its weakest link. Recruiting a strong team starts with recruiting strong team players.

Red Flags

In addition to the qualities already discussed, it's important to look for red flags when recruiting potential leaders. In *Purpose-Driven™ Youth Ministry*, Doug Fields has identified the following red flags to watch for:
- "a brand new Christian or a person new to your church
- a history of short-term commitments
- a critical spirit
- going through a major life crisis or transition (for example, death of a family member, divorce or separation, major career change)
- high expectation for staff to be best friends or for ministry to provide personal experiences (for example, a thirty-nine-year-old lonely, need-a-life single)
- hidden agenda—desires and expectations that are counter to your values or goals
- not committed to a lifestyle above reproach
- unsupportive spouse"[2]

I would add a few other red flags to Doug's list, such as a past criminal history, a negative or unhealthy relationship with their teenage children, or a desire to relive their teenage years. A potential volunteer is not automatically excluded by having one of these red flags; it just means that caution and further examination are needed.

In his book *Feeding & Leading*, Kenneth Gangel makes the point that "people rarely perform above the level at which they were recruited."[3] In other words, keep your standards high as you seek to recruit the right people to work with your students. It may limit the number of potential candidates, but in the end, it will be well worth it.

How to Recruit

Now that you've thought through some guidelines regarding the kind of people you'd like to recruit, let's look at how to go about recruiting them. Because every ministry situation is different, not every idea that I'm about to suggest will work in your specific context. The goal is *not* for you to implement every idea in this chapter, but rather to stimulate your thinking and planning as to how to effectively recruit leaders. As mentioned earlier, recruiting is hard work. There are no quick fixes or magical cures for recruiting; prayer, persistence, and patience are required.

Pray for More Leaders

The first thing to do when recruiting leaders is to pray. Jesus gave his disciples the following instructions: "The harvest is plentiful but the workers are few. Ask the Lord of the harvest, therefore, to send out workers into his harvest field" (Matthew 9:37-38). Unfortunately, prayer is often the last thing we do when we're trying to recruit leaders. Too often we pray after everything else has failed; we treat prayer as a last ditch effort for help. Yet that's not what Christ had in mind when he told us to pray for more workers.

Prayer is critical to our recruiting efforts because it acknowledges our dependence on God. Rather than putting confidence in our abilities or skills, prayer reminds us that God is the provider of all things, including youth leaders. Pray with confidence that God will be faithful to provide the leaders you need. Pray for things such as wisdom, direction, who and where to recruit, and increased dependence on God. Pray before, during, and after you start recruiting.

Develop an Awareness of the Youth Ministry

Before you start actively recruiting leaders, it's often helpful to develop a church-wide awareness of the youth ministry. Focus on spreading the word, but not just about the need for more leaders; instead focus on what God is doing in and through the youth ministry. When people are aware of the great things God is doing in the youth ministry, they are more likely to want to offer support and help.

Here are some ideas for developing an awareness of the youth ministry in your congregation:

• *Pulpit announcements.* A general announcement will most likely not result in enlisting more leaders, but it will lay the groundwork for creating an awareness of the needs of the youth ministry. Make it positive, meaningful, and personal.

• *A youth ministry table.* Set up a youth ministry table in a visible place such as the church lobby. Include photos of students, upcoming events, brochures, business cards, and information on how to get involved. Consider having a student or volunteer host the table during the peak traffic hours or during the key recruiting months.

• *Interviews and testimonies of youth leaders.* In front of the church, bring up leaders to share their stories of how God is using them in the youth ministry. You can prerecord them on video or do a live presentation. Because many adults believe that in order to work with youth, they need to be young, energetic, self-confident, and have lots of free time, it is important to not showcase only leaders who reinforce this stereotype. In addition to interviews and testimonies, you can also have a volunteer write an article for the church newsletter about the joys of working with youth. If you don't have a church newsletter, consider sending out a separate letter to members of the church. The goal is to address their misconceptions of what it takes to work with youth, as well as highlight the joys of making a difference in the lives of students.

> *Because many adults believe that in order to work with youth, they need to be young, energetic, self-confident, and have lots of free time, it is important to not showcase only leaders who reinforce this stereotype.*

• *Dramas, videos, or slide shows.* Utilizing drama and other multimedia approaches is also a powerful way to connect with others emotionally. Pictures are worth a thousand words. You could have students perform a drama for the church about the importance of youth ministry or show a slide show with pictures of youth leaders ministering to students. If drama or technology isn't your area of strength, ask someone to help you. Either way, don't be afraid to utilize the power of the creative arts.

Develop a List of Potential Leaders

Next, begin gathering a list of potential youth leaders you'd like to recruit. The more people on your list, the better. Even if you think they will turn you down, put them on the list anyway. God has a habit of surprising us. A good place to start collecting recommendations is from the following people:

• *Church leaders* (elders, deacons, pastor, influential lay leaders). Church leaders typically have a good understanding of church members who demonstrate the character and ability to work with youth. They will also likely know a longer history of how each member has served in the church in the past and may be able to identify red flags you're not aware of.

• *Existing youth leaders.* Because the leaders who are already in place know what it takes to work with students, they can help direct you to people who may make good candidates as future leaders. Because they have adult connections within the church through adult Sunday school classes, small groups, and others ministries, they can help expand your list of potential volunteers.

• *Students.* Teenagers might see things adults don't see when it comes to searching for potential leaders. Students are usually very perceptive in recognizing adults who relate well to them and are interested in getting to know them. Ask students which adults they identify as positive role models and would welcome as youth leaders.

• *Parents of teenagers.* Parents care about who works with their children, so they're usually a good source for recommendations. Because many youth workers don't have teenagers of their own, parents are able to see things most youth workers don't. Collecting recommendations from parents is not only a good practice in recruiting leaders, but it also builds parental support because you've sought their opinion and wisdom.

After you've gathered your list, pray through the list and ask God for discernment and wisdom as to whom you should approach and when. Try to learn as much as possible about each person ahead of time—that info will help you a lot when you begin recruiting.

Recruit in Advance

Desperation makes us do stupid things. If you try to recruit leaders to sign up right *now*, you'll most likely scare them away. While leaders are always needed, recruiting team members three to six months in advance takes the pressure off them and allows them plenty of time to think through and make a decision about their commitment. You may even want to target certain dates as starting points for leaders to officially join the ministry, such as January, June, or September. Knowing the number of leaders that you need will influence your long-range recruiting goals. At a minimum, you should have at least one adult per eight students. If your youth ministry uses small groups or plans to grow, then a ratio of one adult per five students is more appropriate. Planning in advance is always a better policy than thinking last minute about how to recruit more leaders. It takes more work up front, but in the end, you and the new leaders will be less stressed and more focused.

Create an Informational Packet

It's important to create an informational packet that you can give to potential leaders. You want potential leaders to be informed on the what, why, where, and how of volunteering. The more informed they are, the better. In the packet you'll want to include a welcome page, philosophy of ministry, description of programs, description of leadership expectations, an application, and a request for references. (Doug Fields has done an excellent job addressing this in his book *Purpose-Driven™ Youth Ministry*. Check out his book for more on this topic.) Make sure every potential volunteer has read through the packet before committing to the youth ministry.

Recruit in Person

Once you've decided who you'd like to recruit, approach them in person. Steer clear of an impersonal letter or flier. If you're not able to make initial contact in person, contact them on the phone in order to set up a meeting. Don't share everything over the phone—just find out if they are interested in helping with youth and if they would be willing to sit down with you and learn how to help.

When you meet together, learn more about the person and find out why he or she is interested in working with youth. Try to identify his or her areas of interest and how he or she desires to help in the youth ministry. Then focus on sharing the vision you have for the youth ministry, rather than just discussing areas of need. In general, people respond better to a vision than to a need; talking about needs tends to elicit guilt, whereas talking about vision tends to evoke passion.

Then focus on sharing the vision you have for the youth ministry, rather than just discussing areas of need. In general, people respond better to a vision than to a need; talking about needs tends to elicit guilt, whereas talking about vision tends to evoke passion.

At the end of the meeting, ask the potential leader if he or she has any questions. If you feel positive about the meeting, ask the person if he or she would like an informational packet.

Have a Potential Leader Observe the Program Before Committing

It's a good policy to have potential leaders observe the youth program at least twice. Trying to rush the process by signing up leaders without first having them interact with the students and observing how the youth program is run will only come back to haunt you. You want your potential leaders to be comfortable with the youth program and fully aware of what they are getting themselves into. During the observation period, allow them the freedom to watch without feeling the pressure to participate. At the conclusion of an observation period, sit down with a potential leader, and ask for feedback about what he or she experienced.

Recruit Parents of Teenagers

Often missing from a volunteer team are parents of teenagers. Youth workers tend to recruit people similar to their age, which typically translates into not recruiting parents. Also, many youth workers suffer from "parentophobia" (a fear of parents). During my first few years in ministry, I had a serious case of parentophobia. It became so obvious that I felt uncomfortable around parents that one of my volunteers asked me why I always relied on her to communicate with the parents instead of doing it myself. It was only after I realized the benefits of having parents on the team that I got over my parentophobia and began to actually recruit parents.

Parents of teenagers can contribute to a youth ministry team in some significant ways. First, when planning the youth calendar, parents on your team will help identify red flags in your planning process, such as charging too much for youth events, scheduling events in a non-family-friendly manner, or other potential concerns parents might have about certain events and programs.

Having parents on your team also protects you from unfair criticism. There have been many times when our ministry was unfairly accused of something, and it was the parents on our team that defended us.

And finally, the overall parental support for the youth ministry will increase when you have parents on your team. Parents talk to other parents, and the more parents you have involved with the youth ministry, the better. Support for the youth ministry increases significantly when the parents on your team are also involved in other areas of leadership within the church. For example, one parent I had on my youth ministry team was also on the elder board. When it came time to propose a new project or ask for additional resources, having him on the elder board made a significant difference. When making requests before the elder board, he could share his firsthand experience, as well as help answer questions.

There are a few important things to keep in mind, however, when recruiting parents of teenagers. First ask the student of the parent(s) how he or she feels about Mom or Dad getting involved in the youth ministry. If the student isn't comfortable with his or her parent(s) being in the youth ministry, find another way to get the parent(s) involved. If the student is comfortable with his or her parent(s) helping out, encourage the parent(s) to give their child space by allowing someone else to discipline their child, allowing their child to travel with other adults when driving to youth events, and not being their child's small group leader.

HOW *NOT* TO INVOLVE PARENTS IN MINISTRY

Unfortunately, there are things we do, intentionally and unintentionally, that hinder parents from getting involved in our ministry. Here are the top ten.

" 10. Forget to plan or think ahead. Call parents at the last minute for help and don't give them an opportunity to say no.

9. Forget to say 'please' when asking parents for help and 'thank you' when they do.

8. Use only college-age volunteers in your youth ministry. Assume parents' wisdom and experience don't mean anything in youth ministry.

7. Give into your parentophobia. Convince yourself and your [team] that avoiding parents is good youth ministry.

6. Keep everything a secret from parents. Make everything a surprise and just expect parents to 'trust you.'

5. Ask only churched parents to help in the youth ministry. Believe unchurched parents don't want to help and that God can't possibly reach them through your youth ministry.

4. Communicate that you know what it's like to parent a teenager. Convey to parents that they don't know what they're doing and present yourself as *the* expert on teenagers. Let parents know that if they just follow your 10 easy steps to parenting teenagers, they can be just like you.

3. Assume that you love [the teenagers] more than their parents do.

2. Take full responsibility for the spiritual nurture of teenagers. Communicate to parents that it's not their responsibility to raise their children in the Lord. Expect them to disregard Bible passages such as Psalms 78:1-7, Deuteronomy 6:4-9, Proverbs 22:6, and Ephesians 6:4.

1. Refuse to admit you are wrong, and fail to learn from your mistakes."

(Excerpted from "Moving Parents Off the Bench" by David Chow. GROUP Magazine, Jan/Feb 2001. Copyright © Group Publishing, Inc., P.O. Box 481, Loveland, CO 80539. Reprinted by permission.)

Recruit a Diverse Team

In addition to recruiting parents, it's also important to recruit a team representing different ages, ethnic backgrounds, and personal interests.

In addition to recruiting parents, it's also important to recruit a team representing different ages, ethnic backgrounds, and personal interests.

On an intergenerational level, it's vital that students see the team represent the different ages within the church. They need to see seventy-year-olds as much as they do twenty-year-olds. Having a team that is all the same age portrays a skewed perception of the church.

They also need to see diversity in ethnic backgrounds. Being exposed to different ethnic backgrounds broadens students' understanding of others, as well as the world they live in.

Finally, it's important to recruit those that have diverse personal interests, whether those interests are computers, sports, music, writing, skateboarding, science, or the creative arts. Because not all students relate to the same adults, having a diverse team increases the opportunities for students to connect with various leaders.

Have Existing Leaders Recruit Others

Oftentimes, the best recruiters are team members themselves. Since they're already sold on working with youth, encourage them to use their enthusiasm and personal testimony to recruit others. Adults expect "paid" youth workers to try to recruit them, but when "volunteer" leaders invite them to serve, they're more likely to respond. In *Unsung Heroes*, Les Christie shares this insight: "When a volunteer speaks to prospective volunteers about working with youth, he can speak firsthand about the demands, the joys, the disappointments, the satisfaction. He knows what it's like to have a job outside of church, and how hard it is to squeeze extra hours out of the week to serve in a ministry. If anyone can empathize with the fears of prospective volunteers, it's him."[4]

Have existing leaders make personal contact with people they think would make good leaders. Ask them to make announcements in their Sunday school classes or small groups about volunteer opportunities. When leaders are needed for one-time or short-term projects, ask existing leaders to help share the burden by recruiting new leaders. After a leader has initial contact with a possible volunteer, it's important for you to connect with the potential leader as he or she explores the possibility of working with youth.

Recruit Leaders for One-Time or Short-Term Projects

While the most effective leaders will be your consistent, ongoing volunteers, that's not always the best place to start. Oftentimes, getting a potential volunteer to just show up at youth group is the most important step of recruiting. Chances are, if a potential volunteer spends time with students, his or her openness to helping will increase dramatically.

One of the ways to do this is through allowing people to volunteer for one-time or short-term projects such as driving for youth events, decorating the youth room, offering their homes for youth meetings, being camp counselors, or providing needed resources. With one-time or short-term projects, it's not necessary to have adults observe the youth program or fill out an application. It's only when they're willing to make a consistent commitment that you'll want to move them through the appropriate process.

Conclusion

Finding the right leaders is hard work, but it's worth it. Why? Because students need caring, committed adults who will love them as Christ loves us. It's worth it because parents trust us to provide quality adults who will model Christlike behavior and encourage wise decision-making. It's worth it because healthy leaders attract more healthy leaders. And finally, it's worth it because God loves our kids more than we do, and he wants only the best for them.

Now What?

1. Commit to praying once a week for more leaders.
2. See if other churches in your community have informational packets that they give to potential youth leaders. If so, collect a few informational packets, look through them, and start planning your own informational packet.
3. At the following meetings, ask people for the names of potential youth leaders:
   • elder and deacon board

• youth team meeting

• parent meeting

• youth group

4. Based on your next few youth events, think through ways you can involve potential leaders in one-time or short-term events.

5. Write down three ways you can better involve parents in the youth ministry.

_____

_____

_____

_____

_____

_____

_____

_____

Team-Builder Questions

1. What's the most difficult part about recruiting new leaders?

2. Why is quality more important than quantity when it comes to recruiting leaders?

3. What qualities are most important when recruiting an adult leader?

4. Why does prayer need to be foundational when recruiting leaders?

5. What are ways we can increase awareness of the youth ministry in our church?

6. How does having a diverse team (age, ethnicity, interests, and parents of teens) enhance ministry to students and families?

7. Who are potential leaders we can approach within the next three months about serving in the youth ministry?

ENDNOTES

1. Taken from *Unsung Heroes* by Les Christie. Copyright © 1987 by Youth Specialties, Inc. Used by permission of Zondervan.
2. Taken from *Purpose-Driven™ Youth Ministry* by Doug Fields. Copyright © 1998 by Doug Fields. Used by permission of Zondervan.
3. Excerpted from *Feeding & Leading*, copyright © 1989 Kenneth O. Gangel. Used by permission of Baker Books, a Division of Baker Book House Company.
4. Taken from *Unsung Heroes* by Les Christie. Copyright © 1987 by Youth Specialties, Inc. Used by permission of Zondervan.

CHAPTER 4

Inspiring
Your Team

"*Where there is no vision,*
the people perish."
PROVERBS 29:18A
(KING JAMES VERSION)

I remember the first time I was introduced to the world of puzzles. A friend of the family brought us a gift. Underneath the wrapping paper was a box with a beautiful picture of mountain scenery. Inside the box were the thousands of pieces that made up this incredible puzzle. Motivated by the sight of the breath-taking picture, my brother and I went to work on putting together all the pieces. Determined to finish this puzzle, we spent hours working diligently until it was completed. I remember feeling so excited when I surveyed the completed puzzle. We were so proud of our work that we left the puzzle intact for several months.

Just like that picture on the puzzle box, the vision we cast for our youth ministry will motivate and inspire team members to work together to accomplish goals. Vision is powerful because it paints a picture of where God wants to take your ministry. Vision is what compels us to accomplish great things for God. In *Doing Church as a Team,* Wayne Cordeiro defines vision this way: "Vision is the ability to see what others may not. It is the capacity to see potential—what things could be. Vision is the ability to see what God sees and the God-given motivation to bring what you see to pass!"[1]

Shortly before ascending to heaven, Jesus cast the following vision for the early church: "But you will receive power when the Holy Spirit comes on you; and you will be my witnesses in Jerusalem, and in all Judea and Samaria, and to the ends of the earth" (Acts 1:8). Driven by Jesus' vision and the power of the Holy Spirit, the early church carried out his vision with passion and determination. Against all odds, the early church became an unstoppable force that transformed the world forever.

Ministries become transformed when they are vision-driven instead of program-driven. Programs don't inspire and motivate people; vision does. All the planning and programming on earth won't account for much if there isn't a God-originated vision behind it. When a youth ministry possesses a vision, it can become a life-changing ministry for God's glory.

The Power of Vision

What makes a vision so powerful and compelling? Here are a few reasons.

A Vision "Fleshes Out" the Church's Mission

A church's mission defines its primary objective or purpose. Instead of being driven by tradition, personality, or programs, the mission keeps the church focused on what it's supposed to be doing. The mission for the church is found in Matthew 28:19-20, the Great Commission. "Going and making disciples" should be the mission of every church. Others, such as Doug Fields and Rick Warren, have included the Great Commandment (Matthew 22:37-40) as part of the mission of the church. Either way, the mission of each individual church is not unique since Scripture defines the same mission for every church. A mission statement is typically very short and comprehensive. For example, our youth ministry mission statement is fifteen words: "To be used by God to transform students and families into committed followers of Christ."

Vision, on the other hand, is unique and specific to each church. Because no two churches are identical in terms of leadership, culture, demographics, and church and community needs, every church will have a different vision. George Barna puts it this way in *The Power of Team Leadership*: "Working together, mission is about participating in the purposes of God's kingdom. Vision distills your unique, small-but-necessary role in doing so."[2]

> **Because no two churches are identical in terms of leadership, culture, demographics, and church and community needs, every church will have a different vision.**

A church's vision complements the church's mission because it "fleshes out" how the mission statement will look at each specific church. A church's vision statement will generally be much longer and more detailed than a mission statement.

Vision Is a Picture of Where God Wants to Take Your Ministry

If a picture is worth a thousand words, a vision is worth a thousand pictures. Vision helps students and adults understand where God wants to take the ministry. Rick Warren's first sermon at Saddleback Church (below) is a powerful example of using vision to paint a picture of the future of the church. Vision is powerful because it portrays an exciting image of what God wants to do in our ministry.

THE SADDLEBACK VISION

It is the dream of a place where the hurting, the depressed, the frustrated, and the confused can find love, acceptance, help, hope, forgiveness, guidance, and encouragement.

It is the dream of sharing the Good News of Jesus Christ with the hundreds of thousands of residents in south Orange County.

It is the dream of welcoming 20,000 members into the fellowship of our church family—loving, learning, laughing, and living in harmony together.

It is the dream of developing people to spiritual maturity through Bible studies, small groups, seminars, retreats, and a Bible school for our members.

It is the dream of equipping every believer for a significant ministry by helping them discover the gifts and talents God gave them.

It is the dream of sending out hundreds of career missionaries and church workers all around the world, and empowering every member for a personal life mission in the world. It is the dream of sending our members by the thousands on short-term mission projects to every continent. It is the dream of starting at least one new daughter church every year.

It is the dream of at least fifty acres of land, on which will be built a regional church for south Orange County—with beautiful, yet simple, facilities including a worship center seating thousands, a counseling and prayer center, classrooms for Bible studies and training lay ministers, and a recreation area. All of this will be designed to minister to the total person—spiritually, emotionally, physically, and socially—and set in a peaceful, inspiring garden landscape.

I stand before you today and state in confident assurance that these dreams will become reality. Why? Because they are inspired by God!

(Taken from *The Purpose-Driven Church* by Rick Warren. Copyright © 1995 by Rick Warren. Used by permission of Zondervan.)

Vision Excites, Motivates, and Inspires Others for Ministry

A mission informs; a vision excites. There is nothing more motivating and compelling than seeing a clear picture of where God wants to take your ministry. You can tell when a church has vision because people are excited and motivated to do great things for God. The reverse is also true; you can tell when a church lacks vision because people are unresponsive and disinterested in doing great things for God. Ministry becomes more of a chore than a calling, a pain instead of a privilege.

Vision is so powerful because it speaks to our hearts. In his book *Visioneering*, Andy Stanley shares: "Vision evokes emotion...A clear, focused vision actually allows us to experience ahead of time the emotions associated with our anticipated future. These emotions serve to reinforce our commitment to the vision....And the clearer the vision, the stronger the emotion."

Vision Fosters Sacrifice and Commitment

Not only does vision create excitement and energy for ministry, it also fosters sacrifice and commitment from others. It's one thing to get excited about serving God, but it's a totally different thing to make sacrifices and commitments for that purpose. People compelled by a vision are willing to sacrifice their time, energy, and even money.

It was God's vision that gave Nehemiah and his team the determination and strength they needed to complete the rebuilding of the walls of Jerusalem for God's glory. They sacrificed their reputations, financial security, and personal safety for the sake of God's vision. Despite the many setbacks, continual discouragements, and ongoing persecution, it was God's vision that kept Nehemiah and his team committed to fulfilling God's purposes. (For more on this, read the book of Nehemiah.)

> *It was God's vision that gave Nehemiah and his team the determination and strength they needed to complete the rebuilding of the walls of Jerusalem for God's glory. They sacrificed their reputations, financial security, and personal safety for the sake of God's vision.*

Vision Brings Focus to the Ministry

Without vision, ministries lack focus and clarity. The second law of thermodynamics essentially says that everything in the universe tends to go from order to disorder (also known as entropy). In other words, things naturally go from organized to disorganized, from clear to confused, or from clean to cluttered. A ministry without vision is at the mercy of others. Instead of being driven by God's plans, the ministry can become driven by every person's separate agenda. Having a clear vision can keep everyone on the same page. It brings a clear focus and fosters unity. When everyone shares the same vision, unity is a natural byproduct; common goals have a much greater unifying effect than common interests. Just consider the incredible unity the early Christians experienced because of their shared vision to go and make disciples for Jesus.

Having a vision also simplifies decision-making. Instead of making decisions in a haphazard manner, vision provides a framework for evaluation and appropriate action. If something doesn't fit within the vision of the church, then you decide against doing it. Because a ministry can't do everything or be everything, vision allows a ministry to prioritize what it will be and what it will focus on. Vision helps a ministry team prioritize their values and determine what is nonnegotiable.

Vision Gives Meaning to Seemingly Insignificant Tasks

Without an overarching vision, people can become easily frustrated with some of the mundane tasks of ministry. Whether it's paperwork, driving the church van, or forgiving the same person every single week, vision brings importance to the unimportant, significance to the insignificant. Andy Stanley highlights the power of vision in *Visioneering*: "It is the difference between filling bags with dirt and building a dike in order to save a town. There's nothing glamorous or fulfilling about filling bags with dirt. But saving a city is another thing altogether. Building a dike gives meaning to the chore of filling bags with dirt. And so it is with vision."

You know when your ministry has vision because everything has significance. Rather than just focusing on the big things, vision encourages us to focus on the little things, too, because they play an important part of the greater vision.

Visionary Teams

Discovering God's vision for the youth ministry is a critical and important task for the leadership team. Every great team is driven by a vision. A team that possesses vision is a mighty and powerful force for God's purpose. Listen to what John Maxwell has to say in *The 17 Indisputable Laws of Teamwork*: "A team without a vision is, at worst, purposeless. At best, it is subject to the personal (and sometimes selfish) agendas of its various teammates...On the other hand, a team that embraces a vision becomes focused, energized, and confident." Underestimating the power of vision will not only hurt the team, but also the students and families you are ministering to. Take seriously the task of helping your team discover their vision and watch God do amazing things.

While discovering the vision is a team undertaking, vision often starts with an individual. Nehemiah was such a man. After hearing that the walls of Jerusalem were broken down, he developed a vision from God to rebuild the walls. From that initial vision, Nehemiah went on and recruited others who shared the vision and helped him expand and refine it.

The same is true for a youth ministry team. The leader of the team will often be the one that first senses God's vision for the ministry and then initiates the process for the team. In fact, the leader will have often already gone through the steps to discovering God's vision that I'll describe in the following pages. It's not that the leader figures everything out before bringing it to the team, but rather that God often works first in the leader and then the team. The team helps expand, refine, and focus God's vision for the ministry.

Discovering the Vision

While not all teams arrive at a vision in exactly the same manner, the following steps are helpful when leading a team toward discovering God's unique vision for their ministry.

STEP 1: Vision and Prayer

Prayer is the starting point for developing vision. If we are seeking God's vision for ministry, then we must go to the source. Prayer puts us on the same wavelength as God and sensitizes us to his will for our ministry. Prayer allows us to experience what is written in Psalm 46:10: "Be still, and know that I am God." Prayer reminds us that we worship

> *Prayer puts us on the same wavelength as God and sensitizes us to his will for our ministry.*

a powerful God and anything is possible with him. As a result, our faith is enlarged, and we discover the freedom to dream big.

After seeing God's vision for rebuilding the walls of Jerusalem, Nehemiah went to God in prayer, saying, "We are your servants, the people you rescued by your great power and might. O Lord, please hear my prayer! Listen to the prayers of those of us who delight in honoring you. Please grant me success now as I go to ask the king for a great favor. Put it into his heart to be kind to me" (Nehemiah 1:10-11, New Living Translation).

The amazing thing about Nehemiah was that he kept praying this prayer for four months! Even though he didn't know all the details of his vision, he kept faithfully praying to God. As the book of Nehemiah records, eventually God answered his prayer, as well as clarified his vision.

Too often we allow ourselves to get so busy in ministry that we fail to pray. It has been said, "If you're too busy to pray, then you're too busy." Take time with your team to pray. If necessary, schedule a separate meeting time for extended prayer.

Pray as a team, both individually as well as corporately. Ask team members to take some time before a meeting to seek God individually regarding where he wants to take the ministry. When the team comes together, spend time discussing what God has revealed to each team member. Then spend time as a group corporately seeking God for wisdom and clarity.

STEP 2: Dream Big

In order to discover God's vision for your ministry, be willing to dream big. Dreaming big means not worrying about what's possible or probable. One of the enemies of vision is dreaming small or limiting dreams to the practical. If your vision is possible without God, then it's most likely not God's vision. In *The Power of Team Leadership,* George Barna makes an important point: "Human vision is quite limiting. We base our vision on what we can accomplish when we maximize our natural talents and skills. God's vision, however, pushes us beyond our capacity to achieve things that can only be ascribed to the work of the supernatural. God is not interested in what we can do; He is interested in what He can do through us when we are willing vessels."[3]

God only gives us visions that require us to step out in faith and depend on his power. I love what Proverbs 19:21 says: "Many are the plans in a man's heart, but it is the Lord's purpose that prevails." Dreaming big means basing your vision not on your abilities or talents but on God's power and sovereignty. It means remembering Jesus' words in Luke 18:27: "What is impossible with men is possible with God." And lastly, dreaming big means not being afraid of change, but welcoming it as a friend.

After spending time in prayer, take time as a team to dream big. Ask each other the following questions without critiquing or criticizing the responses.

- If money was no object, how would we do youth ministry differently?
- If manpower was unlimited, what new ministries would we start?
- If anything was possible, what would you like to see God do in and through the youth ministry?

If money was no object, how would we do youth ministry differently?

You may also want to give the questions to your leaders ahead of time and allow them to "chew" on them before the meeting. Either way, give your team the freedom to dream big and imagine the impossible. And make sure to write down all of the team members' "big dreams" so you don't forget them.

STEP 3: Question the Status Quo

Vision often develops in reaction to a problem or need. Scripture records Nehemiah's obvious dissatisfaction with the status quo: "They said to me, 'Those who survived the exile and are back in the province are in great trouble and disgrace. The wall of Jerusalem is broken down, and its gates have been burned with fire.' When I heard these things, I sat down and wept. For some days I mourned and fasted and prayed before the God of heaven" (Nehemiah 1:3-4).

A vision is unlikely to develop until a team is discontent with the status quo. As long as the team is comfortable with things the way they are, vision is likely to be far away. Discovering God's vision means not being afraid to question the way things have always been. It means not being afraid of the following questions:

- Why are we doing what we are doing?
- What missed opportunities are we not seeing?
- Where have we let past successes keep us from trying new things?
- Where are the "ruts" or ineffective patterns in the youth ministry?
- What needs or concerns are we not meeting in the youth ministry?
- What needs or concerns in the community are we not meeting through the youth ministry?

Don't be afraid of what you hear. Discontentment can be a powerful way for vision to develop. As long as the comments are constructive and not aimed personally at anyone, encourage team members to share their perspectives. Use a poster board to write everything shared.

STEP 4: Assess the Team

Praying, dreaming big, and questioning the status quo will bring up a lot of issues, but where vision becomes specific is how these issues relate to team members' individual gifts, passions, and talents. Because a team can't do everything or have the passion to do everything, they need to discern where God wants them to focus their energies. Ask the team how they see their gifts and passions relating to the vision of the youth ministry. Each person will have a unique perspective on what excites him or her and how that person sees his or her gifts and talents fitting in. What will result is an awareness of the types of students the ministry is best fit to minister to, what needs the ministry will focus on, and what programs and events will give them the maximum impact.

Step 5: Explore What God Is Doing in Other Ministries

While this is not a necessary step, it can be very helpful to see what visions God is giving to other ministries. The goal here is not to copy someone else's vision, but to see what visions from other ministries resonate with your team members. Vision is often easier to identify when you see it in another ministry than when you have to create it from scratch. Expose your team to other ministries through books, tapes, videos, conferences, and seminars. If possible, take your team to visit other ministries to learn what unique vision God has given them.

Step 6: Seek Feedback From Others

Seek feedback from people you trust and value. Individuals such as the senior pastor, key leaders, parents, spouses, and other youth workers are ideal people to get feedback from. Don't look for a consensus, but instead look for confirmation that you're on the right path. If you discover that several of the people you ask bring up concerns or questions, it would be a good idea to work together as a team to evaluate those concerns and possibly re-evaluate the vision.

Step 7: Enjoy the Process

Vision isn't something we invent; it's something we discover. Because God has a specific vision for each ministry, our role is to discover what that vision is. Discovering God's vision is both a *process* and a *product*. In other words, the process to arrive at the vision is just as important as the destination of understanding the vision. In most cases, developing a vision isn't something that happens overnight, but instead occurs over months of

> **Vision isn't something we invent; it's something we discover.**

prayerful, deliberate, and focused effort.

Allow the team plenty of time to process God's vision for the ministry. Don't feel pressured to produce a well-oiled vision overnight. Good things always take time. There are no shortcuts when it comes to discovering God's vision for your ministry. Many of the ideas presented in this chapter will most likely not happen in one meeting or even a weekend retreat. It's important to keep working at it until God's vision is clear for the ministry.

Sharing the Vision

Sharing the vision is just as important as discovering the vision. While discovering the vision is more beneficial for the team, sharing the vision is more beneficial to the students and families. Sharing the vision will not only reinforce the vision for the team, but it will also provide direction and clarity for the students, parents, and the members of the church.

Write It Down in Its Entirety

Articulating the vision is a critical first step of sharing it. Many visions die at this stage because they weren't translated into an easy-to-read and understandable statement. While the vision statement doesn't need to be as brief as the mission statement, it needs to be as clear and concise as possible. Others should be able to read the vision statement and easily understand what it's saying. You probably don't want it to be longer than a page or two, because if it gets too long, it's not as friendly for readers. In addition to writing with clarity, use words that convey feeling. Vision statements should evoke emotions and inspiringly paint a picture of where God wants to take the ministry.

Display It

Find creative ways to display the vision statement. Enlarge it and put it on a poster or frame it. Print it on a bookmark or a business card. Whatever you do, make sure you put it in a visible place where it will be seen regularly by students and parents. Try to create phrases or slogans that are related to the vision, and use those on posters or notecards. Try to regularly include the vision in the youth, parents', and church's newsletter. The more often you display the vision, the more likely people will be to remember it and think about it.

Talk About It

The most effective way to share the vision is to tell others about it. You can do this through selecting and performing a drama for the church that emphasizes the vision. Students could also create a video that captures the essence of the vision. Testimonies or interviews with students who illustrate the vision are another powerful way to communicate vision. The most powerful method to communicate vision, though, is sharing it with people one-on-one. Encourage team members to share the vision with as many people as possible. Word of mouth is always more effective than mass media.

Teach It

Take time to teach teenagers about the vision of the youth ministry at least once a year. The summer and fall are key times to teach about vision because of all of the new incoming students. Take a different approach or focus every time you teach on the vision so that it doesn't get too repetitive. At your parents' meetings, spend time explaining the vision for the youth ministry and how they are a part of it. If you get an opportunity to preach in the main service, teach on the vision statement of the youth ministry. If that's not possible, ask your senior pastor to teach on it. The more often you teach about vision, the more seriously your students, staff, and parents will take it.

Live It

Most important, the team members need to live the vision. When team members don't live the vision, it demoralizes and discourages students and parents. If the vision involves reaching non-Christian friends, then the team members need to model that in their relationships with adults. If being a servant-leader is part of the vision, then leaders need to model servanthood in action. Team members need to walk their talk. Encourage team members to keep each other accountable to the vision and to help each other overcome their struggles with living it out.

Conclusion

Vision is a powerful thing, but it's also a fragile thing. Just as it takes work to discover the vision, it also takes work to preserve the vision. Through history, people have laughed at and ridiculed people of vision such as Thomas Edison, Abraham Lincoln, Albert Einstein, Orville and Wilbur Wright, and especially Jesus Christ. It takes determination, commitment, and faith to keep a vision alive. Keeping the vision alive in the hearts of the team and students you're ministering to is a never-ending responsibility. Remember the words of Proverbs 29:18, "Where there is no vision, the people perish" (King James Version). When ministries lack a vision to follow God's purpose, they become ineffective and lifeless.

Now What?

1. Schedule a day to spend in prayer and solitude.

2. Plan your next team meeting with a vision-planning focus.

3. Expose your team to other ministry visions by having them listen to tapes or read books.

4. Ask the artistic team members to design a creative way to display your vision.

5. Ask students who are examples of the ministry's vision to share their testimony.

6. Start a four-week teaching series on your ministry's vision in June or September.

Team-Builder Questions

1. How does God's vision differ from people's visions?

2. Where have you seen vision work powerfully in a church or ministry?

3. Where have you seen a lack of vision hurt or weaken a ministry?

4. If anything was possible, what would you like to see God do in and through our youth ministry?

5. What unique passions and abilities do we each bring to the ministry that might contribute to the vision of the ministry?

6. What are specific ways we can begin to share the vision with others inside and outside our church?

7. What changes do we need to make as a team in order to model God's vision to others?

ENDNOTES

1. *Doing Church as a Team* by Wayne Cordeiro. Copyright © 2001. Regal Books, Ventura, CA 93003. Used by permission.
2. Reprinted from *The Power of Team Leadership*. Copyright © 2001 by George Barna. Used by permission of WaterBrook Press, Colorado Springs, CO. All rights reserved.
3. Reprinted from *The Power of Team Leadership*. Copyright © 2001 by George Barna. Used by permission of WaterBrook Press, Colorado Springs, CO. All rights reserved.

CHAPTER 5

Understanding Your Team

"We can learn a great deal about ourselves and others when we explore the various temperaments and their behavioral types…Ministry involves working with all kinds of different people and behavioral styles. By identifying our behavioral styles and the styles of others, we have the potential to increase ministry effectiveness."

AUBREY MALPHURS,

MAXIMIZING YOUR EFFECTIVENESS

When my wife and I first met, we were like oil and water. At first glance it appeared that we had many similarities. We were the same age and went to the same college. We both liked talking and reading, and we were both interested in science and medicine. Upon a closer examination, though, we discovered that our differences far outweighed our similarities. She was friendly and easygoing, whereas I was intense and passionate. She liked routine and stability, while I liked change and variety. She avoided conflict, whereas I thrived on it. She liked working behind the scenes, while I liked being up front. She was more practical and focused on the here-and-now, whereas I was a dreamer and focused on the future. It wasn't exactly a match made in heaven.

We found a lot of truth in the statement "Opposites attract and then they attack." Early on in our relationship, we had many disagreements and conflicts over how we viewed life and people. We realized that our differences would either be a source of strength or stress. The good news is that during the four years we dated, we learned to appreciate each other's differences instead of being frustrated by them. Now having been married for nearly ten years, we've come to see our differences as a blessing instead of a curse.

Teams are much like marriages. Personality differences can be a source of great strength or tremendous stress. When team members don't learn to appreciate and understand each other, miscommunication and conflict will inevitably occur. Even when team members share a common church, community, and love for youth, their differences can be a source of potential problems. Instead of their differences being a source of strength, they can become a cause of division and conflict. Great and effective teams not only appreciate differences in team members, but also come to view their differences as complementary and a source of strength. Rather than letting differences "break" the team, they let them "make" the team.

Understanding the DiSC[1] Profile

When seeking to understand people, our tendency is to look at people through the lenses of our own personalities. It's natural for us to assume that others think, feel, and act like we do. Problems arise when reality doesn't meet our assumptions. The truth is that God has given each of us a different personality. Helping the team understand how each team member's personality contributes to the team is key to overcoming misunderstanding and encouraging unity. When a team member understands his or her unique personality, it not only empowers that person, but it also strengthens the team as a whole.

When a team member understands his or her unique personality, it not only empowers that person, but it also strengthens the team as a whole.

A helpful tool in understanding different personalities is the DiSC inventory. Originally invented in the 1920s by psychologist William Martson, the DiSC system has gone through several revisions since. Each letter in the DiSC inventory stands for a primary personality style: Dominance, Influence, Steadiness, and Conscientiousness. While other inventories, such as the Myers-Briggs Type Indicator, also point out personality styles, the DiSC inventory is more helpful in identifying working styles and potential team conflicts. While everyone has a primary personality style, the reality is that all of us have varying degrees of each style. As I describe each personality style, recognize that I'm making generalizations, and in no way am I attempting to put people into a box. The DiSC inventory is simply a useful tool to help team members understand each other better. As you read the following characteristics of each DiSC style, think through where each member of your youth ministry team fits—and remember, personalities are usually some combination of the following styles.

Dominance Style

Team members who are high in dominance ("high D") respond to their environment by overcoming challenges and achieving results. Being results-driven, they take initiative and seek to make things happen now. Because they challenge the status quo, they enjoy debating and advancing change. They enjoy challenges and are good problem-solvers. They prefer to be in charge, make quick decisions, and are comfortable confronting others. They tend to evaluate everything in terms of the bottom line or end result.

HIGH "D"

Basic Motivation:
- Challenge
- Choices
- Control

Environment Needs:
- Freedom
- Authority
- Varied activities
- Difficult assignments
- Opportunity for advancement

Responds Best to a Leader Who:
- Provides direct answers
- Sticks to business
- Stresses goals
- Provides pressure
- Allows freedom for personal accomplishment

Needs to Learn That:
- People are important
- Relaxation is not a crime
- Some controls are necessary
- Everyone has a boss
- Verbalizing conclusions helps others understand them better

(Excerpted from *Positive Personality Profiles,* copyright © 1993, 2000 Robert A. Rohm, Ph.D. Reprinted by permission of Personality Insights, Inc., Atlanta, GA. For more information, log on to www.personalityinsights.com or call toll free 1-800-509-DISC.)

The strengths of high D's can also be their weaknesses. Because of their desire to manage the environment, they can be overly controlling and independent. Being more task-driven and forceful, they can overwhelm others and be insensitive to people's needs and feelings. Because they are generally impatient and make quick judgments, high D's tend to be poor listeners. Since they make quick decisions, they may fail to involve others in the decision-making process. Last, high D's tend to overuse confrontation, creating unnecessary conflict.

A good example of a high D in the Bible is the Apostle Paul. Prior to becoming a Christian, we see Paul's high D style in his zeal and intensity in persecuting the early church (Acts 9:1-2). After becoming a Christian, we see his high D tendency in his ability to plant new churches, as well as help new churches solve problems. We also often see Paul forcefully confronting others, such as in Galatians 2 when Paul confronts Peter for withdrawing from eating with the Gentile Christians. In Acts 17:16-34, we see Paul debating with the Romans regarding who God is. Finally, in Acts 15:36-41, we see a hint of Paul's insensitivity as he refuses to allow John Mark to travel with him because of a previous failure. (Later on in 2 Timothy 4:11, we see that Paul has changed his opinion of John Mark when he asks Timothy to bring John Mark to him.)

High D's add value to the team when they are given a specific area to develop and expand. They enjoy new challenges and solving problems. They also like freedom from control and supervision. Rather than being told how to do something, they would prefer to be told what needs to be done and be allowed to figure out how best to accomplish it. They relate best to people who give direct answers and boil things down to the bottom line.

Influence Style

Team members who are high in influence ("high I") respond to their environment by seeking to influence others. They tend to be outgoing, friendly, people-oriented, persuasive, and optimistic. Being intuitive, they tend to focus more on the future than the present. Because they are naturally enthusiastic and expressive, they are good at motivating and communicating with others. Being creative and spontaneous, they like variety and having fun. They enjoy being up front and entertaining others.

Again, the strengths of high I's can also be their weaknesses. Because they are spontaneous, they can act impulsively by not thinking through things. Since they're naturally enthusiastic and easily excited, they can tend to overreact to situations. Being socially oriented, they can allow the opinions of others to influence their behavior. Since they're people-focused, they can lose track of details and fail to complete tasks. Their expressiveness can cause them to dominate conversations by talking too much.

A good example of a high I in the Bible is Peter. Naturally enthusiastic, Peter was always eager to talk about Christ. In Acts 2, we see God using Peter to communicate and persuade others when sharing the

---

HIGH "I"

Basic Motivation:
- Recognition
- Approval
- Popularity

Environment Needs:
- Prestige
- Friendly relationships
- Opportunities to influence others
- Opportunities to inspire others
- Chance to verbalize ideas

Responds Best to a Leader Who:
- Is a democratic leader and friend
- Provides social involvement outside of work
- Provides recognition of abilities
- Offers incentives for risk-taking
- Creates an atmosphere of excitement

Needs to Learn That:
- Time must be managed
- Too much optimism can be harmful
- Listening is important
- Tasks must be completed
- Accountability is imperative

(Excerpted from *Positive Personality Profiles,* copyright © 1993, 2000 Robert A. Rohm, Ph.D. Reprinted by permission of Personality Insights, Inc., Atlanta, GA. For more information, log on to www.personalityinsights.com or call toll free 1-800-509-DISC.)

---

gospel with those gathered for Pentecost. We also see some of the weaknesses of high I's in Peter's life. In Galatians 2:11-13, we see that Peter withdrew from associating with Gentiles due to the social pressure of the Christian Jews. As mentioned earlier, it was Paul, the high D, who confronted Peter about this. Peter's impulsiveness (which is both good and bad) can be clearly seen in some of his spontaneous and thoughtless comments, in his jumping out of the boat to meet Jesus, and in his cutting off the high priest's ear during Jesus' arrest.

High I's add value to the team when they can be in front of others. They are good at welcoming others and creating a fun and enjoyable environment. They can help a team think outside of the box with their creativity and imagination. They respond well to change and are good at thinking on the fly. Last, their verbal skills and enthusiasm make them good sources of inspiration and motivation for others.

Steadiness Style

Team members who are high in steadiness ("high S") respond to their environment by working together with others to accomplish tasks. They are easygoing, patient, and good listeners. They like to help others by working behind the scenes and prefer participating in a group rather than leading one. They seek stability and routine and maintain the status quo. They are consistent in their work habits and are good at completing tasks. They are loyal in their friendships and are good at keeping others' confidences. They tend to focus on the present and are more practical in their orientation.

Like the other personality styles, high S strengths are also weaknesses. With their emphasis on maintaining relationships, they can tend to avoid conflict. Seeking stability and routine, they are slow to adopt change and struggle with increasing the pace of their work. Because they prefer for others to initiate, they can be indecisive and may struggle with starting something on their own. Being low-key and unassuming, they can have difficulty expressing their feelings and thoughts.

A good example of a high S in the Bible is Abraham. Because of Abraham's concern for righteous people, he pleaded with God to not destroy Sodom and Gomorrah. Throughout Genesis, we see Abraham demonstrating hospitality to various people. In Genesis 13, we see Abraham resolving a dispute between Lot and himself concerning sharing the land. Rather than risking his relationship with Lot, he maintained

HIGH "S"

Basic Motivation:
- Security
- Appreciation
- Assurance

Environment Needs:
- An area of specialization
- Identification with a group
- Established work pattern
- Stability of situation
- Consistent, familiar environment

Responds Best to a Leader Who:
- Is relaxed and amiable
- Allows time to adjust to change in plans
- Serves as a friend
- Allows people to work at their own pace
- Clearly defines goals and means of reaching them

Needs to Learn That:
- Change provides opportunity
- Friendship isn't everything
- Discipline is good
- It is all right to say, "No!"
- Being a "servant" does not mean being a "sucker"

(Excerpted from *Positive Personality Profiles,* copyright © 1993, 2000 Robert A. Rohm, Ph.D. Reprinted by permission of Personality Insights, Inc., Atlanta, GA. For more information, log on to www.personalityinsights.com or call toll free 1-800-509-DISC.)

harmony by allowing Lot to choose the land for himself. On the negative side, we see Abraham in Genesis 12 lying about his wife, Sarai, and saying she was his sister in order to avoid opposition and conflict. And when strife occurred between Sarai and her maidservant Hagar, Abraham chose not to intervene.

High S's add value to the team when they are focused on caring for and helping others. As good listeners, they are adept at calming excited people by allowing them to share their thoughts and feelings. Since they are willing to work behind the scenes, they are very loyal to those they believe in. They are willing to perform necessary routine tasks and are good at completing assignments. They also help provide support and stability to the team.

Conscientiousness Style

Team members who are high in conscientiousness ("high C") respond to their environment by conscientiously striving toward excellence and precision. Because they are motivated by accuracy and order, they tend to be cautious and focused on quality control. Being good

---

HIGH "C"

Basic Motivation:
- Quality answers
- Excellence
- Value

Environment Needs:
- Clearly-defined tasks and explanations
- Sufficient time and resources to accomplish tasks
- Team participation
- Limited risks
- Assignments that require planning and precision

Responds Best to a Leader Who:
- Provides reassurance
- Maintains a supportive atmosphere
- Provides an open-door policy
- Defines concise operating standards
- Is detail-oriented

Needs to Learn That:
- Total support is not always necessary
- Thorough explanation is not always possible
- Deadlines must be met
- Taking a calculated risk can be profitable
- There are varying degrees of excellence

(Excerpted from *Positive Personality Profiles,* copyright © 1993, 2000 Robert A. Rohm, Ph.D. Reprinted by permission of Personality Insights, Inc., Atlanta, GA. For more information, log on to www.personalityinsights.com or call toll free 1-800-509-DISC.)

---

with details, they are objective and analytical thinkers. They like clearly defined expectations and responsibilities and work well within structure and hierarchy. They dislike taking risks and sudden changes that might threaten quality control.

Weaknesses of high C's are also related to their strengths. Due to their high standards and need for accuracy, they can be perfectionistic and nit-picky. Having an objective and analytic mind-set, others can perceive them as aloof and impersonal. Because they dislike taking risks, they may pass up unique opportunities. Preferring clearly defined expectations, they can tend to resist change and innovation.

A good example of a high C in the Bible is Luke. In writing the book of Luke, he makes these opening remarks: "Therefore, since I myself have carefully investigated everything from the beginning, it seemed good also to me to write an orderly account for you" (Luke 1:3). Luke goes to great effort to maintain historical and chronological accuracy within his gospel account. Luke, believed to be a doctor, was a careful and exact historian. As a result, Luke felt a great need to write an orderly and precise account of Jesus' ministry and the early church.

High C's add value to the team when working with details and facts. When considering a change, high C's can help the team think through all the potential problems and needed details. They are good at creating policies and structures that ensure quality control. They are also willing to perform tasks if they are clearly defined.

Using the DiSC

After gaining an understanding of the different personality styles, it's helpful to have the team take a DiSC inventory. The inventory will be a more precise measurement tool and will help team members to identify more complex combinations of the different styles and how they interact. To purchase DiSC inventories, you can contact Inscape Publishing, Inc. at www.inscapepublishing.com. Sonlife Ministries, a Christian organization dedicated to helping churches and youth ministries fulfill the Great Commission, offers both the DiSC inventory and a team-building manual. The team-building manual is a helpful tool for the team after they have taken the inventory. These resources can be ordered by calling 1-800-770-GROW or visiting www.sonlife.com.

Applying the DiSC

Helping team members understand each other's personality styles will result in the team valuing each other's differences, as well as relying on each other's strengths. Rather than seeing personality differences as good or bad, team members will come to appreciate what each personality style brings. A positive way to facilitate this is by having team members share what they've noticed as the personality strengths of each team member. Not only is this affirming to team members, but it also brings to the surface the positive contributions of each team member. Encouraging team members to see things from each other's perspective is another helpful way to increase sensitivity and awareness of personality differences. When a high I realizes that a high S needs stability and predictability, it helps him or her to realize that not everyone likes change and spontaneity. When a high D realizes that a high C needs time to process and think, it helps that person slow down and be more patient with others.

Helping team members understand each other's personality styles will result in the team valuing each other's differences, as well as relying on each other's strengths.

Another important way to apply the DiSC inventory is to help team members identify potential team conflicts related to personality differences. When team members understand how their behavior creates frustration with others, it can help them avoid potential conflict with other team members. When conflict does occur, the DiSC profiles can provide a framework to help resolve any misunderstandings or miscommunications.

And last, encourage team members to address their weaknesses related to their personality style. Personality differences should never be an excuse for bad character or un-Christlike behavior. In order to become more like Christ, it's important for team members to allow God to transform their personality weaknesses. Paul reminds us of this in 2 Corinthians 5:17, writing, "Therefore, if anyone is in Christ, he is a new creation; the old has gone, the new has come!"

Conclusion

Your own DiSC personality style will influence your style of leadership. The good news is that there is not one personality style that is best for leading. God has used leaders with vastly different personality styles to accomplish his will. If you're a high D, your strength will be your determination and focus on results. Overcoming challenges and getting things done will come more naturally to you. Your weakness will be impatience and insensitivity to others.

If you're a high I, your strength will be your personal charisma and optimism. Persuading and getting others involved will come more naturally to you. Your weakness will be a lack of attention to details and not having a practical strategy to accomplish your goals.

If you're a high S, your strength will be your concern for and sensitivity to others. Listening to and caring for others will come more naturally to you. Your weakness will be avoiding conflict and difficulty initiating change.

If you're a high C, your strength will be your attention to details and ability to thoroughly analyze situations. Maintaining quality control and creating a structured environment will come more naturally to you. Your weakness will be being a perfectionist and lacking flexibility when it comes to new situations.

Regardless of personality style, God can use you to lead effectively. The question isn't "Do I have the right personality style?" but "How can I maximize my personality strengths and minimize my weaknesses?"

Now What?

1. Have your team take a DiSC inventory, and spend time processing the results.

2. Have the team share what they see as personality strengths of each team member.

3. Assign team members roles and responsibilities that fit their personality styles.

4. Have team members with different personality styles work together on a project.

5. Have team members openly discuss personality conflict and misunderstandings between each other with the objective of facilitating understanding and resolution.

Team-Builder Questions

1. How could using the DiSC inventory prevent conflicts or misunderstandings between team members?

2. If you haven't taken a DiSC inventory, what's your best guess about your own personality tendencies?

3. In what ways does the DiSC help explain things about you?

4. Based on your DiSC style, what strengths do you bring to the team? What are areas in which you'd like to grow?

5. In what ways does your DiSC style shape the way you minister to students?

6. How does your DiSC style influence the way you lead others?

7. How does understanding each other's DiSC style strengthen our team?

ENDNOTES

1. The term "DiSC" and DiSC descriptions from *Personal Profile System*, copyright © 1994 by Inscape Publishing, Inc., reprinted by permission of Inscape Publishing, Inc. Minneapolis, MN 55426.

Connecting Your Team

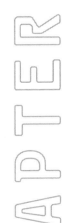

"*All the believers were together and had everything in common. Selling their possessions and goods, they gave to anyone as he had need. Every day they continued to meet together in the temple courts. They broke bread in their homes and ate together with glad and sincere hearts, praising God and enjoying the favor of all the people. And the Lord added to their number daily those who were being saved.*"

ACTS 2:44-47

Sam. Frasier. Woody. Norm. Cliff. Carla. Rebecca. Remember them? On the air for eleven seasons, this TV "family" from *Cheers* typified the real meaning of community for its thousands of loyal fans. Set in a bar in Boston, the group of friends in *Cheers* always seemed to come through for each other. Despite their enormous differences in personality, background, vocation, and ideology, they possessed a deep loyalty and commitment to one another. The show's theme song, "Where Everybody Knows Your Name," said it all; the Cheers bar was a place where lonely people could feel valued by and connected with friends.

The popularity of *Cheers* had much to do with what it offered: the hope of friendships that are deeper than simply common interests or common paths. Long before *Cheers* ever aired on TV, God designed the church to exemplify such genuine and deep relationships. As Christians, our connection is stronger than friendship, marriage, or even blood. It's a spiritual connection that happens through trusting and following Christ. Galatians 3:26-28 teaches us this: "So you are all children of God through faith in Christ Jesus. And all who have been united with Christ in baptism have been made like him. There is no longer Jew or Gentile, slave or free, male or female. For you are all Christians—you are one in Christ Jesus" (New Living Translation).

Unlike the crew in *Cheers*, what the church shares in common is faith in Jesus Christ. As a result, Jesus prayed specifically for the church to be connected and unified as one, saying, "My prayer is not for them alone. I pray also for those who will believe in me through their message, that all of them may be one, Father, just as you are in me and I am in you. May they also be in us so that the world may believe that you have sent me. I have given them the glory that you gave me, that they may be one as we are one: I in them and you in me. May they be brought to complete unity to let the world know that you sent me and have loved them even as you have loved me" (John 17:20-23).

As part of the church, God desires that leadership teams model for others what it means to be "connected in Christ."

As part of the church, God desires that leadership teams model for others what it means to be "connected in Christ." Teams lead by example when they practice unity and teamwork.

Team Diagnosis

How can you tell whether a team is connected or disconnected? Teams that are not connected are unmistakable. Disconnected teams suffer from the following problems:

- Interactions have a high degree of formality and politeness.
- Disagreements are rarely raised, and conflict is avoided.
- There is little give and take among team members.
- Members don't like spending time with other members outside the group time.
- Team meetings are quiet, anxious, and generally uncomfortable.
- Members leave as soon as possible and rarely stay around after the meeting.
- Attendance at meetings is inconsistent and unpredictable.

Just as it's easy to spot a disconnected team, it's also easy to spot a connected team. The signs of connected teams are also unmistakable. They display the following characteristics:

- Team members demonstrate a high degree of comfort and informality when interacting.
- Team members are able to kid around and make jokes with each other.
- Team members feel comfortable being noisy, "spastic," and random.
- Meetings often run overtime, and people stay around afterward.
- Disagreements between team members are voiced and received nondefensively.

• Team members like spending time with each other outside meeting times.

• Attendance at meetings is consistent, and team members rarely miss meetings.

Advantages of Connected Teams

Not only is being connected to each other biblical, it's also the most effective way to function as a team. Here are a few of the advantages of developing a highly connected team.

Higher Morale

One of the undeniable traits of a connected team is high morale. Everyone generally feels good and is ready to tackle anything. Teams that have high morale have a positive attitude and are open to new challenges. They pull together when they're under pressure and are more resistant to discouragement and frustration whereas low morale teams often suffer from waning commitments and internal strife.

The Academy Award–winning movie *Braveheart*, starring Mel Gibson, is an incredible picture of high morale. Despite being vastly outnumbered by the English army, the Scottish rebels led by William Wallace fought with passion and fierceness. Because of the conviction of their cause and their commitment to one another, they amazingly managed to defeat the English army.

Greater Longevity and Less Turnover

Unlike disconnected teams that experience high turnover, connected teams grow deeper and stronger over time. When people leave a team that's well connected, it's rarely out of frustration or dissatisfaction. Experienced leaders Kenneth Gangel and Dennis Williams explain, "A positive team spirit among workers produces greater commitment to the ministry, less absenteeism, greater longevity in service, and people who are fulfilled in ministry."[1] A positive sign of a connected team is the longevity of team members; a high turnover rate is a clear sign of a disconnected team. Keep your team connected, and you'll *keep* the team.

Enhanced Communication and Group Participation

Connected teams are able to be honest and straightforward with each other. Having moved beyond the formality and politeness stage, connected team members can share what's really on their hearts and not be afraid of being misunderstood. The level of participation is increased because everyone feels comfortable contributing his or her opinions and ideas. When (not if) conflict occurs, connected teams can talk through the issues and come to a positive resolution without permanently damaging their relationships with one another.

In Acts 6, we learn of a dispute in the early church between the Grecian Jews and Hebraic Jews concerning food distribution to widows. The following is the response of the early church's leadership team: "So the Twelve gathered all the disciples together and said, 'It would not be right for us to neglect the ministry of the word of God in order to wait on tables. Brothers, choose seven men from among you who are known to be full of the Spirit and wisdom. We will turn this responsibility over to them and will give our attention to prayer and the ministry of the word.' This proposal pleased the whole group" (Acts 6:2-5a).

When an issue arose that could have easily caused division and distracted the early church from its focus on the mission, the church leaders openly discussed the issue at hand. As a result, they arrived at a solution that satisfied everyone.

> *When an issue arose that could have easily caused division and distracted the early church from its focus on the mission, the church leaders openly discussed the issue at hand. As a result, they arrived at a solution that satisfied everyone.*

Stronger Group Loyalty

Group loyalty is at an all-time high in connected teams. Team members have a strong commitment to each other and are willing to make sacrifices for one another. Group loyalty motivates stronger team members to come alongside and help weaker team members. Loyalty is the "glue" of every strong and healthy team. When loyalty exists in a team, team members are faithful to one another because they know that others will reciprocate the same faithfulness. Loyalty is what enables teams to stick together through both the good and bad times.

During Christ's time on earth, the disciples continually failed at displaying loyalty to each other. Jealousy, mistrust, and independent spirits were common behaviors among the disciples. But after Christ's departure, the disciples' loyalty to one another became the foundation for the early church. Despite intense persecution, rejection, and discrimination, they remained faithful to Christ and each other.

Increased Productivity

Connected teams accomplish more, overcome more challenges, and outperform disconnected teams. Productivity is viewed as a team effort, rather than an individual's responsibility. Success is defined by what the team accomplishes, not just by what an individual achieves. In addition, connected teams are more effective at brainstorming and sharing ideas with each other.

The U.S. Air Force did a study trying to determine what was the best predictor of improved flying performance. While they assumed that increased flying experience would result in increased flying performance, they were surprised to find out that "the time a crew spent flying together was a far more accurate predictor of improved performance than was individual flying experience."[2] In other words, pilots' performance increased as they became more connected to each other through flying together.

In the book of Nehemiah, we see an awesome example of the productivity of teams working together to accomplish God's purposes. While facing continuous ridicule, oppression, and physical harm, Nehemiah's team successfully and powerfully rebuilt the walls of Jerusalem. What for many would have been only an impossible dream became a reality as a result of a committed and connected team of individuals.

Increased Spiritual Growth

Being on a connected team not only benefits the team, but it also benefits each individual team member. People who feel connected with others experience personal and spiritual growth. We see this clearly in Acts 2 as the early Christians spent time together, sharing everything with each other and devoting themselves to prayer. Engaging in genuine and life-transforming fellowship, the early Christians experienced incredible spiritual growth as God used them to change the world. The same experience is possible today for a team-centered youth ministry. Team members can experience close fellowship and accountability with other Christians and be naturally encouraged to grow in their relationships with Christ. When teams are connected, team members grow spiritually. And when your team grows spiritually, so do the students in your ministry.

> *When teams are connected, team members grow spiritually. And when your team grows spiritually, so do the students in your ministry.*

Connecting the Team

Connected teams don't happen by accident. They happen through intentional and deliberate action. The following are keys to developing a connected team.

Connect Through Shared Experiences

There was a common saying in the '90s that "quality" time was more important than "quantity" time. People applied this principle to parenting, relationships, and even working out. The reality is that both quantity and quality are important. Quantity time in and of itself is not enough, but neither is quality time. When it comes to connecting teams, you want to encourage and provide both quality and quantity time. One of the best ways to do this is through providing shared experiences for the team. Here are a few ideas for shared experiences that you can organize for your team.

• PRAYER AND SHARE

Allowing team members to share what's going in their lives, as well as providing time to share personal prayer requests, is a simple but often overlooked connecting experience. Whether it's before or after youth group, during staff meetings, or between team members, be intentional about encouraging prayer and sharing.

• SHARING MEALS

Another simple way to connect the team is to share meals together. Sharing meals was a common practice for the early church. There's just something about eating together that facilitates connectedness. Restaurants work well, but having a potluck or sharing a meal at a team member's house is even more powerful.

• TEAM SOCIALS

A team social event is another simple way to spend time together and improve the connectedness of the team. Getting together to play games, watch a movie, or barbecue are just a few ideas. Our youth ministry team tries to get together at least once a quarter for a social gathering, and we usually rotate from one team member's house to the next.

• HAVE FUN TOGETHER!

You've heard the statement "Families that play together stay together." When it comes to teams, "Teams that play together stay together." Doing something out of the ordinary and just plain fun is a powerful shared experience. Find out what the team enjoys, and plan an event out of it. One of the most enjoyable things our team did together was playing paintball. We challenged a youth ministry team from another church and had a blast getting splattered for Jesus. If paintball doesn't work for you, try water or snow skiing, miniature golf, rock climbing, laser tag, or if you're really crazy, bungee jumping.

• TEAM RETREATS

While they require extra planning, team retreats are a powerful way to connect your team. Similar to a youth retreat, you'll want to include times for team building, worship, prayer, and training. Make it a priority to plan at least one team retreat a year. Good locations are rental cabins, hotels, or retreat centers. If you can't spare an entire weekend, do a Friday night to Saturday night retreat. The key is to pick a date far enough in advance so that every team member can go.

• JOINT OUTSIDE ACTIVITIES

If the team has the time, a great way to connect a team is to have members engage together in an outside activity such as a sports league or some other common interest. One youth ministry team I know of joined a softball league and had a great time competing together. Other ideas might be taking a class together or working on a joint project such as repairing a house or landscaping a yard.

Connect Through Team Building

In addition to shared experiences, team building is another effective way to connect teams. Team building develops the group's identity and strengthens team members' commitment to one another. Here are some ways you can facilitate team building.

• ESTABLISH A TEAM COVENANT

Creating a covenant is a powerful way for the team to develop ownership and unity. A covenant is a verbal or written agreement of the expectations, practices, goals, and behaviors that a team decides for the group. Unlike a contract that is conditional and restricting, a covenant is an intentional commitment of team members to each other. George Cladis in *Leading the Team-Based Church* explains it this way: "The goal of the covenant is not to delineate specific behaviors in such a way that the agreement feels like a straight jacket. Rather the covenant is meant to give order to passion, to set forth respectful and honorable ways of living forth one's heartfelt love."[3]

A covenant provides a guide for the team's purpose and goals. It also keeps the team accountable when team members break the covenant. A covenant typically takes one to two meetings to complete. The time frame isn't as important as the team's sense of ownership of the covenant. It's important that everyone on the team feels free to share his or her opinion and perspective. While it's not necessary to create a new covenant every year, it's important to update and revise it when appropriate. The following questions are helpful in guiding a team in the development of a covenant.

Purpose of group—What's our mission and vision for the ministry?

Participation—What level of participation are team members expected to give based on their roles and responsibilities?

Caring—How will we care for and encourage one another?

Communication—Will we be honest, genuine, and transparent with each other? Or will we be closed, inauthentic, and protective?

CRYSTAL CATHEDRAL STUDENT MINISTRIES TEAM COVENANT

1. We will remember we are a ministry, first and foremost.
2. We will work to get along and promote encouragement through seeing the positive in situations.
3. We will keep a sense of humor and laugh with each other.
4. Teamwork needs to be learned as well as earned; it's not a right or a privilege.
5. Success is measured by what the team accomplishes.
6. We will support each other in public and deal with problems in private.
7. We will give grace freely by not keeping a record of wrongs.
8. We will have fun team building every week.
9. We will give each other the benefit of the doubt.
10. We will seek to communicate openly and honestly with each other.
11. We will be sensitive with joking around and will seek to use other forms of communication besides sarcasm.
12. We will be respectful of each other's time, energy, and personal boundaries.
13. We will appreciate each other's differences and complement one another with our strengths.
14. Because none of us is perfect, we will all strive to improve even in our own strengths.

Problem solving—How will we deal with conflict and disagreement?

Confidentiality—How will we keep each other's secrets and other private information confidential?

Accountability—In what ways will we "speak the truth in love" to each other?

Prayer—When and how often will we pray for each other?

After completing the covenant, write it down, and have each team member sign it. Make copies of the covenant for current and future team members. Display the original in a public place for team members to see. Have the team review the covenant often, revise it when needed, and reward team members when they follow it. (See page 82 for an example of the covenant our youth ministry team has created.)

• TEAM-BUILDING EXERCISES

Team-building exercises are a fun way for the team to connect. Youth groups have been doing them for years. The following are my favorites.

Human Knots—Everyone stands in a circle, and each person reaches across to grab the hand of another person. After everyone is attached, the group tries to "unknot" themselves without breaking hold of each other. If you want to emphasize the importance of communication, don't let team members talk during the exercise.

Trust Walk or Trust Fall—Team members partner up and take turns being blindfolded. The blindfolded partner in each pair must hold his or her partner's hand and trust the partner to lead him or her on a walk through several obstacles. A trust fall is when a blindfolded team member stands on a chair (or platform about four feet tall) and falls backward onto the arms of the group below.

Electric Fence—Using a rope as an imaginary electric fence about five feet off the ground, team members must help get the entire team over the fence without touching the fence. They cannot go under the fence or touch the poles or objects the rope is attached to.

Ropes Courses—Ropes courses encourage team members to trust one another, conquer their fears, and overcome new challenges. They typically take a few hours to complete and are best experienced with a professional guide.

In addition to the ideas presented, a great resource for more team-building ideas is *Building Community in Youth Groups* by Denny Rydberg (Group Publishing, Inc.). Make sure to spend some time debriefing after each team-building exercise. Encouraging team members to share their experience is a powerful way to connect a team.

• SPEND TIME WITH INDIVIDUAL TEAM MEMBERS

Spending time with individual team members indirectly facilitates team building. A leader who meets individually with team members is better able to understand the needs of each team member and how he or she relates to the group. In addition, team members may use those opportunities to share with the team leader concerns and issues that they aren't ready to share with the group. As they become more comfortable sharing with their leader, they will eventually become comfortable sharing with the team.

Developing Teamwork

In addition to team building, helping the team understand and experience teamwork is an effective way to develop connectedness on the team. Here are a few ideas to help you do this.

• THINKING LIKE A TEAM

The first step in developing a connected team is to help team members think like a team. This means encouraging team members to substitute the word *we* for *I*. Helping team members to define success by what the team, not the individual, accomplishes is another way to think like a team. Prompting team members to share in each other's successes and especially failures also facilitates a team mentality. Thinking like a team is strengthened when team members see and understand the necessity of working together to accomplish God's vision for the ministry.

• TEAM SYMBOLS

Creating team symbols, logos, or mottoes is another great way to develop teamwork. I experienced this many years ago when I worked at a Christian camp as a lifeguard. The big movie at the time was *The Untouchables*, starring Kevin Costner and Sean Connery, and so we named our lifeguard team after the title of the movie. After ceremoniously decorating a wooden oar with paint and our signatures, we proudly hung it in the boathouse for all to see. A simple way to do this with a youth ministry team is to work together to design a staff T-shirt. Another great idea is to put a team logo or symbol on a hat, sticker, or coffee cup. If there's room in your budget, these would be great appreciation gifts to give to team members.

• DISCOVER TEAM STRENGTHS

Just as every team member has unique strengths, every team has strengths unique to the group. Every team is strong at something, whether it is leading small groups, planning special events, team teaching, or reaching out to high-risk teenagers. Helping a team find out what its own unique strengths are builds team pride. Help the team to discover its strengths by discussing it as a group or spontaneously complimenting the team for various jobs well done.

• PRACTICE TEAMWORK

Providing opportunities for the team to work together is an effective way to build a sense of connection. A great way to do this is to give the team tasks and responsibilities that require teamwork, such as planning a special event, organizing a retreat, or building a house as a service project. Just like any skill or ability, teamwork improves with experience and practice.

• SETTING TEAM GOALS

Encouraging the team to prayerfully set goals for the youth ministry is a positive way to promote teamwork. Some examples of goals to consider are how many students will be discipled, the number of outreach events, and how many students will become leaders in a given time period. Goals can be short-range (one to six months), medium-range (six to twelve months), and long-range (one year and beyond). Goals need to be clearly stated and easy to measure.

• CELEBRATING TEAM SUCCESSES

When the team succeeds at something, celebrate it! Celebrating team accomplishments is a powerful way to reinforce the value of teamwork. What made Southwest Airlines the number four company in Fortune magazine's 2001 list of Best Companies to Work For was their unrelenting commitment to celebrate team successes. They developed a corporate culture of celebration, regularly staging parties (and documenting them) to honor company and employee successes. Whether it's taking the team out to dinner, purchasing special gifts, or giving everyone high fives, find fun and creative ways to celebrate success. Go ahead and party!

> *Whether it's taking the team out to dinner, purchasing special gifts, or giving everyone high fives, find fun and creative ways to celebrate success. Go ahead and party!*

Address Team Problems

Just as important as shared experiences, team building, and developing teamwork is the importance of addressing team problems. *Every* team will encounter problems. When teams can't face their problems, the problems only get worse. Like a fast-growing cancer, team problems eventually become unmanageable and sometimes irreparable. When divisive issues aren't dealt with properly, team members experience tension, anxiety, and a loss of ministry focus. Church growth expert Gary McIntosh shares some of the consequences of working in an unhealthy team situation in *Staffing Your Church for Growth*, saying, "Hostile team situations are very harmful to the individual and the church. Team members who have served in such negative situations report that they lost time worrying about avoiding the instigator and about future interactions...At least half gave serious thought to resigning their positions and between 10 and 20 percent did resign to get away from the difficult work experience."[4]

Rather than being focused on the mission and vision of the ministry, a team can become consumed and divided by its problems. So this doesn't happen to you, make it a priority to identify and properly deal with the following team problems.

• UNRECOGNIZED AND UNRESOLVED CONFLICT

Conflict in itself isn't bad, but unrecognized and unresolved conflict is. When conflict is dealt with properly, it can be a source of growth and understanding for the team. Consider what veteran pastor and expert team builder Harold Westing had to say in the *Church Staff Handbook*: "There are numerous benefits of having conflict. In fact, without it there will be little productivity and little growth in the skill of functioning as a group...Various authors go so far as to suggest that the absence of conflict within a group is often the indication of a powerless group."[5] In other words, the goal shouldn't be to remove conflict from the team, but to help team members resolve conflict positively.

Conflict happens for a number of reasons, such as misunderstanding, selfishness, insecurity, or external events. How people respond to conflict is also varied. People typically respond to conflict by fighting back, giving in, avoiding it, or working through it. While there are times when fighting back, giving in, and avoiding conflict is appropriate, in general, the best approach is to work through it by resolving it positively.

An acronym I've created for conflict resolution is the CLEAR method.

C—CLARIFY THE PROBLEM

Help team members separate the person from the problem. Encourage team members not to take everything personally, and discourage counterattacking. The question you want addressed at this stage is "Why are we in conflict?"

L—LISTEN CAREFULLY

Encourage team members to listen carefully to each other. Too often we worry about what to say next instead of focusing attention on what the other person is saying. Seek first to understand the person before seeking to be understood. Encourage team members to assume the best about each other and clarify what they're hearing. The question you want addressed at this stage is "What do you see as the problem?"

E—EXPRESS FRUSTRATION

While you don't want team members to vent uncontrollably, it is valuable to encourage team members to share their feelings openly and honestly. Discourage negative behaviors such as pouting, giving the silent treatment, or taking low blows. Encourage team members to use "I" language instead of "you" language. For example, sharing, "You let me down," is not nearly as helpful as sharing, "I felt let down." Likewise, saying, "You rejected me," is not as effective as saying, "I felt rejected." The question you want addressed at this stage is "What feelings do we need to share?"

A—AGREE ON A SOLUTION

Assuming team members have been successful at clarifying the issue, have listened carefully to each other, and have expressed frustration positively, the next step is to brainstorm possible solutions. The goal is to arrive at a win/win solution where both parties are satisfied. The question you want addressed at this stage is "What solution can we both agree on?"

R—RESOLVE AND BE READY FOR FUTURE CONFLICT

At this point, resolution has been achieved. Encourage team members to forgive each other and put the past behind them. Also help the team to understand that conflict is a never-ending reality and, if dealt with properly, it can be a positive and growing experience for everyone involved.

Keep in mind that there are times it is more beneficial for the leader to not intervene in conflict. See the sidebar to the left for a helpful list of questions to ask yourself when deciding on whether to get involved in a team conflict.

• SUBGROUPING

Another common problem is when team members form subgroups within the team. Similar to cliques in youth groups, subgrouping fosters competing allegiances. Rather than having a unified team, subgrouping creates a divisive and competitive environment. When subgrouping occurs, help team members identify the problem, and encourage them to work it out. If that doesn't work, have team members from different subgroups work together on a common project. If the problem can be traced to a single team member, confront the team member, and give him or her the option to solve the problem or step down from the team.

• SCAPEGOATING

A final common team problem is when team members begin blaming each other for their problems and failures. It's always easier to blame someone for your problem than it is to take responsibility. Help team members learn from failure instead of looking for ways to cast the blame on others. As a leader, model for the team what it means to take responsibility for your actions and especially your failures. If a specific team member consistently blames others for his or her problems, meet privately with that person and speak the truth in love.

Conclusion

Being connected is the foundation for an effective and dynamic team. Being a connected team is not only practical, but it is also spiritually rewarding. When our teams are connected in Christ, we are living out Jesus' desire for unity among his followers. Being a connected team brings honor to God and inspiration to others. Remember Jesus' words in John 13:34b-35, "Love each other. Just as I have loved you, you should love each other. Your love for one another will prove to the world that you are my disciples" (New Living Translation). There is no more powerful way to prove to our students that we love Christ than when we love each other. The proof is in the pudding.

Now What?

1. Spend fifteen minutes during the next staff meeting doing a team-building exercise, followed by fifteen minutes of prayer and sharing. (For team-building ideas, see page 83.)

2. Plan a fun team event such as laser tag, go-karts, or miniature golf.

3. Schedule a team meeting to focus on developing a covenant.

4. Schedule a one-on-one "checkup" with each team member.

5. Have the team design a staff T-shirt to wear at youth group.

6. Pick a recent team success, and find a creative way to celebrate it.

7. Teach the CLEAR method to the team members.

Team-Builder Questions

1. Based on what you read about connected or disconnected teams, which type best describes our current team? Why?

2. Which advantage of having a connected team means the most to you?

3. What's something fun we could do together as a team on a regular basis?

4. In creating a covenant, what key issues do we need to address as a team?

5. As a team, what makes us unique and strong?

6. What are team successes that we need to celebrate more often?

7. What are some possible team problems that we might need to address?

ENDNOTES

1. Excerpted from *Volunteers for Today's Church*, copyright © 1993 Dennis E. Williams and Kenneth O. Gangel. Used by permission of Baker Books, a Division of Baker Book House Company.
2. From *The New Art of the Leader* by William A. Cohen. Copyright © 2000. Reprinted with permission of Prentice Hall Direct.
3. *Leading the Team-Based Church*, George Cladis, copyright © 1999 by George Cladis. Reprinted by permission of John Wiley & Sons, Inc.
4. Excerpted from *Staff Your Church for Growth*, copyright © 2000 Gary L. McIntosh. Used by permission of Baker Books, a Division of Baker Book House Company.
5. Taken from *Church Staff Handbook* © 1985, 1997 by Harold J. Westing. Published by Kregel Publications, Grand Rapids, MI. Used by permission. All rights reserved.

"Effective leaders know that you first have to touch people's hearts before you ask them for a hand…You can't move people to action unless you first move them with emotion. The heart comes before the head."

JOHN MAXWELL,

THE 21 IRREFUTABLE LAWS OF LEADERSHIP

It has been said, "People don't care how much you know until they know how much you care." While often quoted, there is tremendous truth to this. Too often in leadership, we think our job is to impress those under us by knowing all the right answers and being an authority figure. Instead of meeting the needs of our team members, we worry more about having our own needs met. True leadership, on the other hand, is about serving and caring for those around us. Jesus modeled this beautifully to his disciples when he washed their feet right before his betrayal and crucifixion. After demonstrating powerfully what it meant to serve and care for others, Jesus said, "I have set you an example that you should do as I have done for you. I tell you the truth, no servant is greater than his master, nor is a messenger greater than the one who sent him. Now that you know these things, you will be blessed if you do them" (John 13:15-17). In a similar way, God is calling leaders to "wash the feet" of those around them by serving and caring for them.

Know the Needs of Your Team Members

The first step in caring for your team is understanding and knowing the needs of each team member. In Proverbs 27:23, Solomon reminds us to "Be sure you know the condition of your flocks, give careful attention to your herds." In other words, leaders need to know how team members are doing and provide continual care. Just as it is important to know the needs of your students, it's also important to know the needs of your team. When a leader loses touch with the needs of his or her team, team members feel ignored and uncared for. But when a leader understands the needs of the team, team members feel loved and cared for. Here are a few ways to keep in touch with the needs of your team.

Commit to Pray for Team Members

Committing to pray regularly for your ministry team members is important for several reasons. What you pray for is what you care about. When you commit to pray for youth ministry leaders, your care and concern for them will increase. God will enlarge your love for others as you pray for them. Prayer also increases your awareness of and sensitivity to your team members. Prayer has a way of opening our eyes to the needs of those around us and helping us see ways we might meet those needs. It always amazes me how God helps me see things I wouldn't have seen if I hadn't been praying, such as sensing a team member's need or identifying an undiscovered area of strength.

Because God answers prayer, it means a lot to our team members when we pray for them. Jesus had a practice of praying for his disciples, whether early in the morning, late at night, prior to his crucifixion, or before departing earth. James 5:16 reminds us of the importance of praying for one another, saying, "Therefore confess your sins to each other and pray for each other so that you may be healed. The prayer of a righteous man is powerful and effective."

It's important that, as you pray for team members, you pray specifically. Take time to ask team members how you can pray for them and keep updated so you adjust your prayer requests. Whether you pray for them daily or weekly, the important point is to pray for them consistently and specifically.

Take Time to Listen

Another way to know the needs of your team members is to take the time to listen. Listening is a lost value in our culture of incessant talking. People are usually praised and recognized for their ability to talk, not their ability to listen. The reality is that your ability to listen will mean more to your team than your ability to speak eloquently or persuasively.

The reality is that your ability to listen will mean more to your team than your ability to speak eloquently or persuasively.

It's *much* more common for me to have team members thank me for listening than for talking. God reminds us of this in James 1:19: "My dear brothers, take note of this: Everyone should be quick to listen, slow to speak and slow to become angry."

Listening communicates respect by demonstrating that you are genuinely interested in how another person is doing and what's going on in his or her life. Because very few people take the time to ask how we are truly doing, taking the time to listen communicates value and high regard. Through listening, you convey to others that you care about their feelings, value their opinions, and are genuinely interested in who they are.

Listening means asking questions with a sincere and genuine attitude instead of making quick judgments or assumptions. There's nothing more frustrating than people failing to understand us because they're not listening carefully. Asking good questions and listening carefully to someone's answers is a powerful way to care for your team members.

Listening means allowing team members the freedom to verbalize their thoughts and feelings without interrupting them or prematurely responding. As a high D (see Chapter 5), I have to work *hard* at allowing team members to share their thoughts and feelings without interrupting them or cutting the conversation short.

Listening means communicating with your body language that you're sincerely interested through making eye contact, leaning forward, nodding, and smiling. Research has shown that our body language communicates far more than our words. If your body doesn't show that you're paying attention, people won't believe you're listening to them.

In the end, listening is more of an art than a science. It's something that you have to learn and continue developing as you lead your team.

Appreciate Team Members

In addition to knowing the needs of your team members, finding ways to appreciate them is another effective way to care for them. When you fail to appreciate your team members, they will end up feeling used and taken advantage of. The more you appreciate the leaders on your team, the more they will feel cared for and loved. You can communicate appreciation to your team in the following ways.

Don't Take Team Members for Granted
Especially when it comes to volunteers, you need to be extra careful to always recognize how valuable they are to you and to the ministry. In *The Care and Feeding of Volunteers*, Douglas Johnson states five helpful

"nots" to remember when working with volunteers.

- "Volunteers are not members of the staff.
- Volunteers are not full-time workers.
- Volunteers cannot be taken for granted.
- Volunteers are not paid.
- Volunteers are not bound to a job in the church for long periods of time."

Because volunteers are not members of the church staff, our authority over them is limited. As a result, you need to work primarily through influence and persuasion, not through demands or orders. Because volunteers are not full-time staff, they don't have forty-plus hours a week to give to ministering to students. Consequently, you need to be sensitive and realistic about the time volunteers can give to students. Because volunteers are not motivated by money, but instead are motivated by the desire to make a difference in the lives of students, you need to help them be successful in reaching and caring for students. And last, because volunteers are not bound to a job in the church for a long time, you need to give them the freedom to move on when they have fulfilled their initial obligation. While we all desire longevity with our volunteers, we need to be sensitive to their needs and desires and send them off with love and appreciation if they choose to move on.

Give Gifts

Another great way to appreciate team members is to give them each a gift. Everyone loves to receive gifts! When someone takes the time to pick out a gift for us, it makes us feel special and appreciated. Oftentimes, the best gifts are ones that cost very little or even nothing. Not too long ago, our ministry celebrated the one-year anniversary of one of our team members by giving her a certificate and prayer locket. The total cost of the items was very little, but the impact on her was huge. Doug Fields likes to tell the story of how he used to buy old trophies at thrift stores for around fifty cents and then spend two to three dollars to have each trophy personalized for the volunteer of the month. Not only was it fun to receive a trophy with a giant bowler or softball player on it, but it meant a lot to the volunteers to receive a tangible "thank you" for their service. Other easy and simple gift ideas are movie passes, books, Christian jewelry, or photo collages.

Another wonderful gift to give is time off. When team members and especially volunteers have served for a long time, short breaks can be a wonderful blessing to them. Whether it's a month off or the whole summer off, giving team members time off will not only bless them, but it will also help the ministry when they come back refreshed and recharged.

Whether it's a month off or the whole summer off, giving team members time off will not only bless them, but it will also help the ministry when they come back refreshed and recharged.

Celebrate Birthdays and Special Occasions

Finally, another simple way to appreciate team members is to remember and celebrate their birthdays. Keeping a list of all the birthdays of your team members and remembering to celebrate them is a powerful way to help them feel appreciated. In addition to birthdays, you might want to celebrate special occasions like wedding anniversaries or their children's birthdays.

Provide Encouragement

The Merriam-Webster Dictionary defines *encourage* as "to inspire with courage and hope." In other words, encouragement is meant to strengthen and uplift others. Long before there were dictionaries, the Bible talked about the importance of encouragement. Paul reminds us of the purpose of encouragement in 1 Thessalonians 5:11, writing, "Therefore encourage one another and *build each other up*, just as in fact you are doing" (emphasis added).

Encouragement is meant to build others up. The role of encouragement is so important that the author of Hebrews instructs us to do it every day, saying, "But encourage one another daily, as long as it is called Today, so that none of you may be hardened by sin's deceitfulness" (Hebrews 3:13).

Unfortunately, encouragement is an essential but missing ingredient in most ministries. Encouragement often becomes an afterthought or something we do as a last resort. Lawrence Crabb and Dan Allender stressed it this way in *Encouragement*: "Encouragement is important business. It merits our careful attention, not only because Scripture tells us directly to think about it, but also because it represents the unique value of Christian fellowship...Encouragement is the kind of expression that helps someone want to be a better Christian, even when life is rough."[1]

When leaders fail to encourage their team members, discouragement and frustration set in. To avoid this trap, make encouragement a top priority as you work with your team. Here are a few simple and practical ways to encourage your team members.

Practice Praise

Praise is a powerful weapon when used for God's purposes. Even researchers have confirmed the power of praise. Hanz Finzel wrote in *The Top Ten Mistakes Leaders Make*, "Organizational researchers have been telling us for years that affirmation motivates people much more than financial incentives, but we still don't get it. People thrive on praise. It does more to keep the people who work for you and with you fulfilled than fortune or fame could do." While team members don't enter ministry for the praise, they value and appreciate it when they receive it. I've never had a team member come up to me and say, "Stop praising me!" The best principle to follow is this: The more praise, the better.

A simple way to practice praise is to thank often. Thanking team members should be a regular event in your youth ministry. Learning to thank team members for the small things is just as important as thanking them for the big things. Doug Fields shared his wisdom in *Purpose-Driven™ Youth Ministry* when he said, "Recognition doesn't have to be saved for the spectacular. There is power in affirming people for their normal and ordinary acts of ministry. Your leaders probably aren't being shown much appreciation by students, so your kind words won't be easily forgotten."[2] Simple things such as writing a note or sending an e-mail go a long way toward thanking someone. Calling team members to say thank you or leaving thoughtful messages on their answering machines is another easy but effective idea. Saying thank you to a team member's spouse or parent is another great way to show your appreciation. Whatever the means, thank often and thank regularly.

Another way to practice praise is to always give credit where credit is due. Oftentimes in youth ministry, parents call us first when something positive happens in their children's lives. Rather than accepting the credit for what one of the team members has done, have the parents contact that person directly to thank him or her. It means so much more when team members hear directly from the parents how much they are appreciated than when they hear it from us secondhand.

Finally, when practicing praise, always praise in public and correct in private. Whether it's acknowledging someone for a specific accomplishment, recognizing one's service, or pointing out how the person is impacting students, praising a team member in front of others communicates that you truly appreciate and value him or her. When you do the reverse—correct in public and praise in private—you damage people's feelings and destroy their confidence. While you can always praise team members in private, correcting team members

> *When you do the reverse—correct in public and praise in private—you damage people's feelings and destroy their confidence.*

publicly only embarrasses and hurts them. When you have to correct team members, make sure to sandwich your correction between praise. In other words, start with praise and end with praise. Because practice makes perfect, mastering the art of praise will be one of the most important skills you develop as a leader.

Believe in Others

One of the most powerful ways to encourage team members is to believe in them. Jesus used this approach powerfully in Peter's life. Despite all of Peter's mistakes and failures, Jesus continued to believe in him. In Matthew 16:13-19, Jesus painted a picture of how God would use Peter to build the church. Even after Peter denied that he knew Jesus, Jesus maintained his confidence in Peter by restoring him in John 21:15-19. Jesus' belief in Peter had an incredible impact on him. Throughout Acts, we see God use Peter in great ways, such as being the first spokesman for the church at Pentecost, performing miracles that led to thousands of people coming to Christ, and being given the vision to share the gospel with the Gentiles. These things might not have occurred in Peter's life if Jesus hadn't believed in him. Believing in others is the highest form of encouragement. Listen to what John Maxwell has to say: "When you believe in people, you motivate them and release their potential. And people can sense intuitively when a person really believes in them. Anyone can see people as they are. It takes a leader to see what they can become…and believe that they will do it" (*Developing the Leaders Around You*). As I look back on my time in ministry up until now, I can see that it was the belief of others that allowed me to keep moving forward despite the discouragement and setbacks I faced. When I needed to raise financial support as an intern, it was the belief of my supporters that affirmed and strengthened my calling for ministry. I remember being in awe of how much others believed in me as they committed to support me financially and with prayer. After accepting my first full-time youth ministry position, it was the belief and confidence of the church's elders and senior pastor that kept me encouraged as I figured out ministry on my own. And when I did make mistakes, they didn't lose confidence in me. Even today, as I continue to minister to students and families, it's the support of my wife, mentors, friends, and, most important, Jesus that keeps me going. When you believe in your team members, you extend Jesus' love and confidence to them.

BELIEVING IN PEOPLE

Here are seven essential principles for believing in others, outlined by John Maxwell and Jim Doran in *Becoming a Person of Influence.*

- "Believe in them before they succeed."
- "Emphasize their strengths."
- "List their past successes."
- "Instill confidence when they fail."
- "Experience some wins together."
- "Visualize their future success."
- "Expect a new level of living."

Support Team Members

Supporting others is another vital part of caring for team members. All of us, at one time or another, need the support of those around us. Team members will know that you really care for them when you commit to be there for them during those difficult times. Paul explained it this way in Galatians 6:2: "Carry each other's burdens, and in this way you will fulfill the law of Christ." When we support team members by sharing their burdens, we are fulfilling Christ's command to love one another as Christ loved us. Support happens through being accessible, being there during times of crisis, and standing by team members when they're facing criticism.

Be Accessible

While you can't be accessible to everyone, it's important to be accessible to your ministry team. When team members can't get ahold of us, it makes them feel unimportant and insignificant. Do whatever it takes to make yourself accessible to your team members. Giving team members your home and cell phone numbers, identifying times they can drop by, or clarifying other ways they can get ahold of you when they need you are simple ways to increase your accessibility. When team members feel that they are at the top of your list, it makes them feel valued and cared for. One of the things I appreciate about my current church is that, despite the large size of our church, my executive pastor is *always* accessible to me. Whether calling him on the phone, scheduling a meeting on short notice, or talking to him after a meeting, I know I can always count on him to be there for me.

Scheduling "one-on-ones" with team members is also a great way to increase your accessibility. Team members feel cared for and supported when you're willing to carve time out of your busy schedule to meet with them. Make the one-on-one an informal time of encouragement, feedback, and support. In my one-on-one meetings with team members, I like to spend time catching up on their personal lives, as well as how things are going with their relationship with God. I make sure to encourage them by sharing where they are making an impact in the youth ministry and how much students appreciate them. When appropriate, I'll give feedback on a specific task or ministry responsibility they're in charge of. Last, I ask how I can better pray for and support them as team members. My goal is to meet with paid staff (interns, directors, assistants) weekly and with volunteers at least once a quarter. Being accessible not only communicates that you care for your team members, but it's also a powerful way to lead by example. When you make yourself accessible to your team, you model to them how they are to relate to students.

Being There During Times of Crisis

Supporting team members means being there for them during the good times as well as the bad times. Every time a team member faces a crisis, it's a critical time for the leader to support and care for that person. Whether the crisis is a death in the family, a broken relationship, or a financial hardship, team members need leaders who will support and strengthen them.

Several years ago, I had a team member who suddenly died from a severe form of leukemia. Not only was it tragic to lose Jason so quickly, but he left behind a wife and two young children. The incredible thing that came out of the tragedy was the

It was exciting to see the church be the church.

amount of support the team and the church extended to Jason's family. Cooking meals, collecting money, finishing home projects left undone, and continually praying were just some of the ways the team and the church family supported them. It was exciting to see the church be *the church*. When you stand by team members during crises, you powerfully communicate your care and love for them.

Standing by Team Members When They Face Criticism

Supporting team members also means standing by them when they face criticism. Criticism is a difficult thing to deal with, but it's even more difficult to face when you're all alone. One of the pastors at my church often says, "90 percent of caring is just showing up." Just being there for someone is a way to show you care. Supporting team members means giving them the benefit of the doubt when you hear something bad about them. Rather than accepting what others say at face value, go directly to the team member and ask if what you've heard is true. If it isn't true, then make sure to defend and protect them. One time I had a team member who was unfairly accused of something he didn't do. It meant a lot to him when I stood by him and did everything in my power to defend and protect him. If the criticism is valid, you need to help team members learn and grow from it. Even when criticism is valid, though, team members need to know that you still believe in and support them. Because team members will make mistakes, it's important that they know you still stand by them even in their failures.

Conclusion

When you care for your team, you are, in essence, shepherding them. Much like shepherds that care for and protect their flocks, God has instructed leaders to care for and protect those they lead. Listen to Peter's words: "Be shepherds of God's flock that is under your care, serving as overseers—not because you must, but because you are willing, as God wants you to be; not greedy for money, but eager to serve; not lording it over those entrusted to you, but being examples to the flock" (1 Peter 5:2-3). When you care for your team, you are being Jesus to them. And by being Jesus to them, you inspire them to be Jesus to the students they care for.

Now What?

1. The next time you see your team members, ask them how you can pray for them.

2. Ask those closest to you to evaluate your listening ability.

3. Begin a tradition of celebrating team members' birthdays.

4. Schedule one-on-one's with each of your team members.

5. Write a thank you note to each team member this week.

Team-Builder Questions

1. Do you agree with the statement "People don't care how much you know until they know how much you care"? Why or why not?

2. What actions and attitudes interfere with your ability to listen to others? What can you do about it?

3. What happens when we take each other for granted? How can we prevent it?

4. What would happen to our team if we praised each other more often? How can you put it into practice?

5. What does it mean for us to believe in each other?

6. How well do we support each other during crisis and criticism?

7. What are practical ways we can show our support for each other?

ENDNOTES

1. Taken from *Encouragement: The Key to Caring* by Lawrence J. Crabb, Jr. and Dan B. Allender. Copyright © 1984 by The Zondervan Corporation. Used by permission of Zondervan.
2. Taken from *Purpose-Driven™ Youth Ministry* by Doug Fields. Copyright © 1998 by Doug Fields. Used by permission of Zondervan.

CHAPTER 8

Training Your Team

"Volunteers need training. Most feel totally inadequate. They're afraid you'll dump them into a roomful of young people and leave them there. They need to be assured that you won't desert or ignore them."

LES CHRISTIE, *UNSUNG HEROES*[1]

I never fully appreciated the need to train others until I was put in charge of a group of Bible study leaders. Because I had figured out how to lead a Bible study, I assumed they would too. So instead of taking the time to train them, I left them to do it on their own. As you can imagine, their Bible studies suffered that year. Not wanting to repeat the same mistake the following year, I decided to learn how to train and equip leaders for ministry. And what a difference it made! It was then that I realized training leaders needs to be a top priority in ministry.

Every youth ministry has an opportunity to be either a training center for leaders or a shopping center for consumers. When a youth ministry's goal is to satisfy consumers, its focus becomes developing programs instead of people. But when a youth ministry makes training and equipping leaders its goal, its focus becomes turning members into ministers, whether they're students or adults. This is what Paul was talking about in Ephesians 4:11-13 when he said, "It was he who gave some to be apostles, some to be prophets, some to be evangelists, and some to be pastors and teachers, *to prepare God's people for works of service*, so that the body of Christ may be built up until we all reach unity in the faith and in the knowledge of the Son of God and become mature, attaining to the whole measure of the fullness of Christ" (emphasis added).

As a leader, God has called you "to prepare God's people for works of service." In other words, your job is to train and equip others for ministry instead of doing all the ministry yourself while others watch. The problem is that very few churches take seriously the need to train their leaders, and this lack of training has negative effects. As Dennis Williams and Kenneth Gangel explain in *Volunteers for Today's Church*, "From interviews and observations, however, it appears that church leaders do not provide adequate training for their volunteers...Many workers are left alone to figure out what is expected and how to fulfill the responsibility. When this happens, volunteers commonly determine their own activities and establish minimally acceptable performance standards."[2] Training team members can't be left to chance; it needs to be intentional and well planned.

Benefits of Training

Effectively training leaders is very rewarding for all those involved. First and foremost, training benefits the team members themselves. When team members experience quality training, it builds their confidence by giving them the skills to be successful in ministry. Jesus was a master at providing training experiences for his followers, as we can see in Luke 10:1, 17: "After this the Lord appointed seventy-two others and sent them two by two ahead of him to every town and place where he was about to go...The seventy-two returned with joy and said, 'Lord, even the demons submit to us in your name.' " After sending his followers out to gain experience and training in ministering to others, they came back joyful and confident. In a similar way, when team members receive helpful training, they feel empowered and confident for ministry.

When team members experience quality training, it builds their confidence by giving them the skills to be successful in ministry.

Another benefit of training leaders is what it does for the ministry as a whole. Training draws team members together as they share a common vision of excellence and effectiveness. Quality training brings into focus where the ministry needs to go and what skills and abilities are necessary to accomplish those goals. Going through training together also provides a shared experience and vocabulary for team members to draw from. Even if team members disagree, they are all still working from the same page. Because training benefits everyone, it's essential that leaders make it a top priority in developing a team-centered youth ministry.

Training Principles

Before discussing the how to's of training, it's important to understand the principles underlying effective training. The following are some principles to keep in mind when training team members.

Training Must Be Intentional

In order for training to happen, it must be intentional. Training team members can't be something that's left to chance. You can't assume that team members will seek out the needed training on their own. As a leader, it's your responsibility to prioritize and plan training as part of your overall strategy for developing a team-centered youth ministry. Effective training always starts with a leader who is intentional and purposeful.

Training Needs to Be Tailored to Your Team

There's no "cookie cutter" approach or "one size fits all" curriculum for training team members. Based on the needs of your ministry, how and what to train leaders will look different from that of other youth ministry teams. For example, if small groups are a significant part of your ministry, then team members need greater amounts of training on leading small groups than youth ministries that only do large group meetings. Likewise, if your group is trying to reach out to unchurched students, it would be wise to spend some time doing training about relating to non-Christian students and effectively sharing the gospel. While there are some basic skills that all youth leaders need, what you cover, how much, and how often will depend on your ministry situation.

> There's no "cookie cutter" approach or "one size fits all" curriculum for training team members.

Balance Skill Training With Personal Spiritual Development

It's important when training team members not to emphasize developing ministry skills over developing one's spiritual life. Because ministry flows out of who we are, it's essential that we nurture the spiritual lives of our team members. Whether this means working through a spiritual development book together, providing opportunities for "solo time" with God, or facilitating extended times of prayer, helping team members grow spiritually is a vital part of ministry training. (See the Recommended Reading section on page 140 for resources on personal spiritual growth.)

Understand the Stages of Training

Training is not a one-time event; it occurs in stages. The first stage is *exposure*. This is when team members are first introduced to new ideas and skills. This stage can be exciting as team members become aware of new concepts and principles. The next stage is *familiarity*. This is when team members become comfortable with the topic being covered. Because they've been exposed to the information before, they now have a foundation from which to draw. The danger at this stage is to confuse familiarity with the final stage, *understanding*. In the understanding stage, team members can apply the training they've learned, and, ideally, they're now equipped to teach others. Effective training is when people are moved through all three stages.

Create a Need for Training

One common tendency is to train team members before creating a need for it. If team members don't sense a need for training, their motivation and enthusiasm will be low. Creating a need for training means moving team members from unconscious incompetence (not seeing that they need help) to conscious incompetence (seeing that they need help). People typically don't recognize their need until after they're in situations in which they feel inadequate. For example, a Sunday school teacher will be much more motivated to get training on teaching after he has taught a few times than before he has even begun teaching. Finding ways to create a felt need for training will greatly enhance your training process.

Training Is an On-Going Process

It's easy to fool ourselves into thinking that we've accomplished all the needed training in a one-day seminar or weekend retreat. Yet the final principle to keep in mind is that training team members is never a finished task; it's a continual process. Not only does training need to be ongoing, but it also needs to be progressive. It's important to start with the fundamentals but then move on to more advanced training topics. The important thing is not to send team members into training overload mode! In our excitement to quench our team members' thirst for training, we can sometimes tend to give them a fire hose instead of a tall glass of water. It's always better to take it slow than to overwhelm them with information.

Training Topics

While every ministry will need to tailor its training to the needs of the ministry, there are certain fundamental skills every youth worker should cover. The following topics will help you get started as you develop a training program.

Connecting With Students

A key skill for team members to learn is how to connect with and care for students. Teenagers are relationally starved, so effective training in this area can equip team members to really make a difference in teenagers' lives. Youth ministries that don't train their team members to connect with students end up with program-based and relationally shallow ministries.

Helping Students Trust Christ

It's also important that team members know how to openly discuss the gospel with a non-Christian student who is interested in making a faith commitment to Jesus. Equipping team members to help a student trust Christ shouldn't involve years of seminary training or extensive Bible knowledge; instead it's best to focus on a simple tool or procedure. We've had great success with training team members to share the gospel with students by showing them how to use the *Knowing God Personally* booklet published by Sonlife Ministries. The booklet is easy to read, straightforward, self-explanatory, and inexpensive. Helpful video curriculums for training students and adults on this topic include Youth for Christ's *Live the Life!* series and *Becoming a Contagious Christian* by Mark Mittelberg, Lee Strobel, and Bill Hybels.

(For more resources on youth evangelism, see the Recommended Reading section on page 141.)

BUILDING HEALTHY RELATIONSHIPS WITH TEENS

- Listen.
- Learn names.
- Show an interest in teens' lives.
- Accept kids as they are.
- Develop a sense of humor.
- Attend events that teens are involved in.
- Initiate, even though it may feel strange.
- Speak naturally and conversationally.
- Be yourself.
- Pray for those kids you are getting to know.
- Communicate your enthusiasm rather than flaunt your doubt.
- Don't force yourself into situations.
- Be prepared to have to earn the right to be heard.
- Be sensitive to boundaries of time, physical contact, emotions, and differences in maturity.

(Taken from *Equipped to Serve: Volunteer Youth Worker Training Course Leader's Guide* by Dennis "Tiger" McLuen. Copyright © 1994 by Youth Specialties, Inc. Used by permission of Zondervan.)

Helping Students Grow Spiritually

In addition to training team members to help students trust Christ, it's also important to help team members know how to assist students in growing spiritually. Team members should know how to teach students how to study the Bible, listen and pray to God, worship God, and serve others. See the sidebar called "Fueling Kids' Faith" (right) for ideas on helping students grow spiritually. (For more resources on this specific topic, check out page 141.)

Understanding Adolescence and Youth Culture

Everyone who works with teenagers needs to have a basic understanding of adolescent development in terms of their physical, emotional, social, intellectual, and spiritual growth. It's also helpful for youth leaders to have an awareness of youth culture and how today's students differ from adults. Magazines such as GROUP and Youthworker journal, as well as the youthculture@today newsletter from the Center for Parent/Youth Understanding, are excellent ways to keep the team updated on what's hot in youth culture. (For some books on youth culture and adolescent development, see the Recommended Reading list on page 141.)

FUELING KIDS' FAITH

1. Challenge them.
2. Forgive them.
3. Expose them to the experiences of others.
4. Ask them to share their stories.
5. Offer them meaningful and varied worship experiences.
6. Teach them who God is.
7. Teach the basics.
8. Invite questions.
9. Teach about other belief systems.
10. Involve them in the church.
11. Help them come to their own conclusions.
12. Encourage youth leadership.
13. Be patient.
14. Stay off the roller coaster.
15. Be honest and straightforward.
16. Affirm the positive.
17. Be an example.
18. Encourage them to express their faith in ways that fit them.
19. Help them make intergenerational connections.
20. Communicate unconditional love.
21. Resist acting shocked by their doubts.
22. Admit you don't know everything.
23. Affirm the sovereignty of God.
24. Stand up for them.
25. Educate adults about kids.
26. Build a safe community.
27. Pray for them.

Leading a Small Group

Students today need positive, healthy small groups. Small groups are where students feel understood, are heard, and are most likely to connect with other students and adults. In smaller youth groups, students can still benefit from having small groups, even if that means having just a guys' group and a girls' group. Even if team members are not leading formal small groups, knowing how to lead a small group will benefit them in other settings. See the sidebar "Ten Commandments for Dynamic Small Groups" (p. 109) for useful ideas on leading successful small groups. (See the Recommended Reading list on page 142 for resources on leading small groups.)

The Training Process

Knowing *how* to train is just as important as knowing what to train about. The following five-step training process is a helpful tool for preparing and equipping team members for ministry. For this example, I'll explain how the process relates to training a team member to lead a small group.

STEP 1: Modeling—I Do It, You Watch

In the modeling stage, the leader asks the team member to observe him or her performing the desired task. In the case of training someone to lead a small group, the leader would ask the team member to sit in on several small group sessions. At this point, the team member only observes and isn't expected to assist. The trainee is encouraged to make mental notes and debrief with the leader after each small group session.

STEP 2: Mentoring—I Do It, You Help

In the mentoring stage, the leader asks the team member to assist with leading the small group. While the leader still plans the lesson, the team member is asked to lead a specific section of the group time, such as the opener, prayer and share time, or asking specific discussion questions. As the weeks progress, the leader increases the team member's role and involves the person more in the planning process.

STEP 3: Coaching—You Do It, I Help

Assuming the team member has seen a healthy example of leading a

TEN COMMANDMENTS FOR DYNAMIC SMALL GROUPS

One: *Thou Shalt Ask Dynamic Questions*

Dynamic questions are open-ended (not answered by yes or no), surface breaking (probe beneath the surface to deeper issues) and thought provoking (not always easily answered)…

Two: *Thou Shalt Realize That Atmosphere Is Everything*

…We need to strive to have an atmosphere filled with unconditional love and acceptance, where students feel safe enough to share what they think and feel.

Three: *Thou Shalt Not Be a Dictator*

Students learn best when they talk—not when you do. Facilitating discussion and interaction is what will help students open up and grow…

Four: *Thou Shalt Not Fill Each Moment with Talking*

It's okay to have silence in the midst of a discussion…Silence can give students time to process and formulate their thoughts and opinions.

Five: *Thou Shalt Be As Transparent and Open As Possible*

We can't ask students to share something that we wouldn't share ourselves…Being open with students frees them to be open with us.

Six: *Thou Shalt Create Tension*

…Tension forces students to think and consider the consequences behind the choices they make, and how those decisions reflect their values and convictions…

Seven: *Thou Shalt Know and Use Scripture*

When dealing with a subject, we should know what the Bible has to say about it…Better to admit that we don't know and find the answer than to give a wrong answer to a tough question.

Eight: *Thou Shalt Always Be Sensitive to the Circumstances*

…Know when to leave what you've planned to talk about and discuss the more urgent felt need of the group…The most important goal is to follow what God is doing in the midst of your small group and get out of the way.

Nine: *Thou Shalt Always Listen Twice As Much As You Speak*

…Those who give kids their ears will capture their hearts and minds. Listen to what students are saying…

Ten: *Thou Shalt Be Their Pastor*

…Know what's going on in students' lives. Pray for your group regularly. Offer encouragement and accountability…

(*The Youth Builder* by Jim Burns, Ph.D. and Mike DeVries. Copyright © 2001. Regal Books, Ventura, CA 93003. Used by permission.)

small group and has been actively involved in leading the small group, the next step is to have the team member lead the small group. In the coaching stage, the leader works behind the scenes to support the team member as he or she leads the small group. Providing valuable feedback and helpful resources is a large part of coaching. This step may also involve the leader helping the team member prepare a lesson or the leader running a small portion of the meeting.

STEP 4: Supporting—You Do It, I Cheer You On

In the supporting stage, the leader moves from being a coach to being a cheerleader. Assuming the team member is becoming competent in leading a small group, the leader's primary role is now to encourage and support the team member. Being there to back up the team member during the small group is a large part of supporting. Writing notes of encouragement, helping the team member learn from failure, and moving forward despite setbacks are all vital parts of supporting team members.

STEP 5: Delegating—You Do It, and Take Someone Else With You

Having developed the competence and confidence to lead a successful group, the team member is now ready to be on his or her own. In the final stage, the trainer should be able to successfully delegate the full responsibility of running the small group to the team member. Just as important, the team member should be able to take another team member through the same training process. In effect, the leader has begun to multiply himself or herself through training new team members.

With each new skill, the steps need to be repeated. Because everyone learns at a different pace, it's important to be sensitive to the needs of the team members by not rushing the process. Even though this progression is straightforward and simple, the most common problem occurs when a leader short-circuits the process by skipping certain steps or progressing to the next step before the previous one has been mastered. Take your time, be patient, and focus more on the person than on the skills being taught.

Additional Training Tools

In addition to the training process, there are several other training approaches that can be helpful for equipping team members.

Vary the Training Formats

Instead of getting locked into one training format, use multiple training formats such as weekend retreats, one-on-one times, all-day workshops, a portion of staff meetings, and monthly training. For example, you could do an August staff retreat followed by short times of training at team meetings and then an all-day workshop in the spring. The key is to find the times that work the best for everyone and vary them throughout the year.

Have Team Members Work Together

Encouraging team members to work together on a project is a great way to connect leaders *and* to enhance training. In addition to increased learning, team members who work together will also benefit from each other's strengths. For example, if one team member is strong organizationally while another team member is strong relationally, their strengths can make a winning combination as they work together on a task or project. When team members learn to work together, training is maximized and learning becomes fun.

> *When team members learn to work together, training is maximized and learning becomes fun.*

Do Field Research

Not everyone learns best from books or lectures. Especially for team members who learn from observation or hands-on experience, field research is a powerful way to bring ideas and skills into focus. Having team members visit other churches, network with other leaders, and personally interview specific leaders are common ways to do field research. It can be very valuable to visit other churches and network with leaders who are modeling what you want your team members to learn and do. Because many cutting-edge churches have their own leadership conferences, many churches will take their entire teams to learn, observe, and dialogue with such churches. Giving team members an opportunity to see ministry outside of their own four walls is a powerful way to expand their learning, as well as open the door to dreaming God's vision for their own youth ministry. Group Publishing has created the Flagship Church line of books in an effort to expose ministry leaders to the principles, ideas, and programs behind several innovative and influential churches. You can find them on the Web at www.flagshipchurches.com.

Attend Conferences, Seminars, and Workshops

Another wonderful training tool is taking your team to a youth ministry conference or seminar. Going to youth ministry conferences has been one of the most powerful training experiences for my team members. When your team has an opportunity to be a part of a conference or seminar, it inspires them as they see other youth workers seeking to be more effective in ministry. It refreshes them as they feel valued and appreciated. It challenges them to reach for a higher level of ministry excellence. Quality youth ministry publishers and organizations regularly provide excellent youth ministry training through conferences and seminars. Likewise, many denominations provide their own training for their churches. While finding the money is always a challenge, don't let a lack of funds stop you from taking your team to a seminar or conference. Whether it means doing a fundraiser, asking church members for a special donation, or requesting scholarships, find creative ways to fund the training and trust God to provide the means.

Youth Ministry Resource Library

Resources are like gold to your team. Most team members, especially volunteers, aren't aware of all the wonderful resources available to them. And those who are aware may not have the money to purchase them. Creating a resource library with youth ministry books, tapes, videos, and curriculum is a great way to enhance the training of your team members. Team members can check out resources as they need them and return them when they've finished.

It's important to purchase books that are practical and have been helpful to other youth workers. You don't want your library stacked with overly theoretical books. A great place to get youth ministry audiotapes is at youth worker conferences. I've cataloged and made available to team members the large number of tapes I've accumulated over the years from the conferences I've attended. In terms of training videos, Youthbuilders has an excellent selection of training videos taught by Jim Burns. You can also point them to helpful youth ministry Web sites such as:

- www.youthministry.com
- www.grouppublishing.com

- www.youthspecialties.com
- www.sonlife.com
- www.youthbuilders.com

Don't feel you need to build your youth ministry resource library overnight. By adding a few books and tapes every year, you'll have a resource-packed library for team members before you know it.

Conclusion

Training and equipping your team members for ministry is not an option; it's a necessity. Not only is it biblical and beneficial, but it follows in the footsteps of Jesus. The master teacher and leader could have spent the majority of his time teaching to the masses, but instead he spent most of his time investing in and training his disciples. While some may have criticized him for ignoring the needs of the many, Jesus knew that by training and developing the few, they would in turn multiply ministry well beyond him. Larry Osborne put it this way in *Growing Your Church Through Training and Motivation*: "It's no accident that Jesus spent the bulk of his ministry training a small group of future leaders rather than an army of foot soldiers. No doubt he knew the future of the church, humanly speaking, depended upon the quality of its leadership." If Jesus had not spent most of his time training and empowering his disciples, the church might never have survived its early days of persecution and oppression. As Jesus demonstrated, a trained team is a mighty force in the hands of God.

Now What?

Evaluate Your Team's Training Level

Based on the following scale, assess your team members' training level. Put a check by the ratings that best fit your team.

	Sufficiently Trained	Have Some Training	Have Minimal Training	Have No Training
Team members have an adequate understanding of youth culture and adolescent development.				
Team members know how to positively connect with and care for students.				
Team members know how to successfully share about Christ with non-Christian students.				
Team members know how to help students grow spiritually.				
Team members know how to lead an effective small group.				

1. Learn more about the youth ministry organizations described in this chapter by visiting their Web sites.

2. Begin creating a youth ministry library by purchasing a few books and tapes.

3. Sign up your team for a youth ministry seminar or conference.

4. Contact your denominational headquarters to find out about denominational youth ministry training resources.

Team-Builder Questions

1. Share an example of how you've benefited from quality training.

2. Which training principle(s) do we need to pay more attention to?

3. In terms of the following training topics (see below), where are we the strongest? Where do we need to improve the most?

- connecting with students
- helping students trust Christ
- helping students grow spiritually
- understanding adolescence and youth culture
- leading a small group

4. What are examples of how we can put into practice the five-step training process mentioned earlier?

5. What would be a valuable church or ministry to visit or network with?

6. What type of youth ministry resources would be most helpful in a youth worker library?

ENDNOTES

1. Taken from *Unsung Heroes* by Les Christie. Copyright © 1987 by Youth Specialties, Inc. Used by permission of Zondervan.
2. Excerpted from *Volunteers for Today's Church*, copyright © 1993 Dennis E. Williams and Kenneth O. Gangel. Used by permission of Baker Books, a Division of Baker Book House Company.

CHAPTER 9

"If your vision is for one year, plant wheat. If your vision is for a decade, plant trees. If your vision is for a lifetime, plant people."

ANCIENT CHINESE PROVERB

Of all the people in the Bible, Moses probably had the toughest job as a leader. Responsible for millions of disobedient and ungrateful Israelites, Moses was put in charge of leading them out of captivity and into the Promised Land. Feeling the burden of this task, Moses soon grew weary: "The next day Moses took his seat to serve as judge for the people, and they stood around him from morning till evening. When his father-in-law saw all that Moses was doing for the people, he said, 'What is this you are doing for the people? Why do you alone sit as judge, while all these people stand around you from morning till evening?'

"Moses answered him, 'Because the people come to me to seek God's will. Whenever they have a dispute, it is brought to me, and I decide between the parties and inform them of God's decrees and laws.'

"Moses' father-in-law replied, 'What you are doing is not good. You and these people who come to you will only wear yourselves out. The work is too heavy for you; you cannot handle it alone' " (Exodus 18:13-18).

The good news is that God provided an answer through Moses' father-in-law. Check out Jethro's wise advice: "Listen now to me and I will give you some advice, and may God be with you. You must be the people's representative before God and bring their disputes to him. Teach them the decrees and laws, and show them the way to live and the duties they are to perform. But select capable men from all the people—men who fear God, trustworthy men who hate dishonest gain—and appoint them as officials over thousands, hundreds, fifties and tens. Have them serve as judges for the people at all times, but have them bring every difficult case to you; the simple cases they can decide themselves. That will make your load lighter, because they will share it with you. If you do this and

God so commands, you will be able to stand the strain, and all these people will go home satisfied" (Exodus 18:19-23).

What Moses learned through the help of his father-in-law was that ministry needs to be shared. More specifically, Moses learned that God desires for leaders to empower others for ministry. Instead of being the end-all and do-all of the ministry, leaders need to empower others to share in the ministry. The final step in developing a team-centered youth ministry is empowering those on the team. While empowering others may be the final step in leading a team, it's also the most important. Empowerment means sharing your influence, resources, opportunities, and experience with others. It's only when people are empowered that they will fully reach their potential.

Empowering others is both an art and a science; it's a science in that the skills of empowering others can be learned, but knowing how to apply those skills takes an artist's touch. Empowerment is different from training. Training focuses on developing skills, whereas empowerment focuses on developing the person. Empowerment is much more than delegation. Delegation is simply transferring a task to someone; empowerment is sharing your author-

Delegation is simply transferring a task to someone; empowerment is sharing your authority and expertise with others in order to help them accomplish God's purposes.

ity and expertise with others in order to help them accomplish God's purposes. Empowerment is developing and releasing people for ministry, not just getting others to help you. In *Leading the Team-Based Church,* George Cladis writes, "Effective ministry teams in the church in the postmodern era are empowering teams. They have put aside the older, hierarchical models and spread out the authority and responsibility of doing ministry. Leadership no longer means taking control, dictating, or giving orders."[1]

When a leader fails to empower others, ministry suffers. Early on in my ministry, I failed to empower a volunteer couple who worked with me. Rather than developing them as co-ministers, I allowed them to remain in the shadows as I did the work of ministry. As a result, I almost lost them as team members. It was only after I took seriously the need to empower them for ministry that they decided to stay involved, and they ended up serving for several more years. When a leader learns to effectively and successfully empower team members, ministry reaches its full potential. Ministry multiplies, leaders are developed, and lives are changed.

Empower Through Investing in People

People are at the heart of empowerment. Empowerment isn't a program as much as it's an opportunity to come alongside people and help them be all that God created them to be. Empowerment only becomes a reality when a leader is ready to invest in others.

Focus on People Instead of Programs

If your goal is to empower others, then people, not programs, need to be your focus. In youth ministry, it's very easy to lose sight of this focus. In *Building Strong People*, Bobbie Reed and John Westfall ask an important question: "Is it our goal to build strong ministries? Or, is it our goal to build strong people who minister? Depending on which of these goals we are committed to, we will automatically allocate our time, energies, and activities in one of two directions: toward completing the task or toward developing people."[2]

Depending on how you answer the above question, the focus of your ministry will be either people or programs. While we'd all like to think that we are focused on developing people instead of programs, reality doesn't always match our assumptions. When you invest in programs, you see results faster and are better able to control your outcomes. But when you invest in people, ministry takes more time and doesn't always turn out the way you thought it would. Bobbie Reed and John Westfall again share their insight: "Leaders who value task completion have the satisfaction of developing and running well-planned programs. The results are clearly and immediately measurable in terms of numbers of meetings, classes or services held, attendance figures, and compliments received...On the other hand, leaders who value developing people may have to wait longer to experience satisfaction...But when we do note the progress and see people changing around us, it is exciting to remember that we had a part in their development."[3]

People, not programs, minister to students. Programs should *always* serve the needs of people instead of people serving the needs of the programs. Don't settle for the short-term benefit of programs when you can experience the lifelong benefit of investing in people. As the ancient Chinese proverb that begins this

> People, not programs, minister to students. Programs should *always serve the needs of people instead of people serving the needs of the programs.*

chapter reminds us, planting people will always take longer, but the results will last a lifetime.

Allow Team Members to Fail

Another aspect of investing in team members is giving them the freedom to fail. If team members don't feel the freedom to make mistakes, they won't be willing to take risks and try new things. As a result, they'll be driven by the fear of failure instead of motivated by the desire for excellence.

Several years ago, I asked one of my ministry team members to plan our eighth-grade graduation party. Although I worked closely with him during the planning process, there were some choices he made that I probably wouldn't have. But rather than stepping in and taking over, I gave him the freedom to experiment. While a few of the things went well, many didn't. Even though he was discouraged at first, he came to value this experience because it allowed him to learn from his mistakes and grow as a leader.

Jesus practiced this same principle in his relationship with Peter. Whether it was asking dumb questions, trying to impress Jesus, denying his Christian faith, or rebuking Jesus, failure was a regular event in Peter's life. In spite of all this, the Scriptures show us over and over again that Jesus gave Peter the freedom to fail and learn from his mistakes. Imagine what would have happened if Jesus had given up on Peter after his first few failures; Peter, quite possibly, might never have become the "rock" that Jesus spoke of in Matthew 16:18.

Allowing team members to fail means extending grace to them when they let you down and encouraging them when they do poorly. Team members feel empowered when they receive love and acceptance despite their failures. Sharing his experience, Hans Finzel said this in *Empowered Leaders*: "People seem to need encouragement most when they sense that they have really failed. Perhaps they failed you, failed the organization, or just failed themselves. In any case, it is at that moment that you as a leader need to show your love."[4]

What team members need to learn from you is that failure is never final. What they do with failure is what really matters. John Maxwell shares this insight in *Developing the Leader Within You*: "Most people think that success is learning how to never fail. But that's not true. Success is learning from failure. Failure is the opportunity to begin again more intelligently. Failure only truly becomes failure when we do not learn from it." Team members are empowered when they no longer fear failure and welcome it as a friend. Like Jesus, we should *never* give up on people, even if they fail and disappoint us.

Help Team Members Establish Personal Goals

Another powerful way to invest in team members is through helping them establish personal goals for ministry. Because every team member joins the team for different reasons, it's important to help team members identify the personal goals that drive them to minister to teenagers. Most leaders forget this and instead try to impose on team members their own goals and desires. Kenn Gangel explains it this way in *Coaching Ministry Teams*: "Don't try to force volunteers to get excited about things *you* want done. Motivation rests in unleashing *their* interests and heartfelt concerns, not imposing the church's agenda."[5] Motivation and ownership result when team members see how their personal goals fit within the larger goals of the ministry. For example, true synergy will occur when a team member realizes that his or her personal goal to reach out to inner-city teenagers fulfills the ministry's vision of ministering to students of all backgrounds and socioeconomic classes.

It's also important to help team members identify attainable goals. If team members set up goals that are unrealistic and unattainable, they'll become frustrated and discouraged. There's a delicate balance required when encouraging team members to have goals that are attainable but are also still challenging enough to stretch them. As they achieve their goals, you should keep encouraging them to establish new and more challenging goals. They may have to "grow into" some of their larger goals by achieving some of their small goals first. Make sure to work with leaders by giving them practical ways to measure progress toward their goals.

Once team members have established personal goals, work alongside them to help them accomplish those goals. Your job as a leader is to help team members become successful. Whether that means providing needed resources, connecting them with the right people, or supporting and encouraging them, you need to do everything in your power to help team members succeed. Empowerment will become a reality when team members experience the satisfaction of achieving their goals and seeing how they benefit the ministry.

Empowerment will become a reality when team members experience the satisfaction of achieving their goals and seeing how they benefit the ministry.

Help Team Members Discover Their Spiritual Gifts

Another important part of empowering others for ministry is helping team members discover their spiritual gifts. As part of the body of Christ, God has given each Christian at least one spiritual gift. Paul talks about this in Romans 12:4-6a, saying, "Just as each of us has one body with many members, and these members do not all have the same function, so in Christ we who are many form one body, and each member belongs to all the others. We have different gifts, according to the grace given us." Furthermore, in 1 Peter 4:10, we are told that our spiritual gifts are meant for service and ministry: "Each one should use whatever gift he has received to serve others, faithfully administering God's grace in its various forms."

It's really a tragedy when Christians fail to discover and use their spiritual gifts for God's purpose. Wayne Cordeiro, pastor of a church in Hawaii, feels so strongly about spiritual gifts that he states, "God has equipped us to serve through the use of our gifts, and if we are unaware of what they are, our ability to serve Him will be immensely impeded. God knew beforehand that His plan to reach the world could never be accomplished by an act of human will; it could only be accomplished through the strength He supplied in the form of spiritual gifts."[6]

One of your main jobs as a team leader is empowering team members to discover, develop, and deploy their spiritual gifts for God's kingdom. It's important to remember that spiritual gifts don't operate in a vacuum; spiritual gifts are influenced by a person's experience, personality, and natural abilities. So as you work to help team members discover and use their gifts, make sure to take these other factors into consideration as well.

While there is a lot of debate regarding the actual number of spiritual gifts and whether certain gifts from the New Testament are still active today, the more significant fact to recognize is that there *are* spiritual gifts. Your viewpoint on spiritual gifts will be influenced by your understanding of Scripture, denominational background, and personal experience. What's important is not to get caught up in the peripheral matters, but rather to focus on helping team members discover their spiritual gifts.

While there is no perfect system for discovering spiritual gifts, the following principles will be useful as you help people discover their spiritual gifts.

Study Spiritual Gifts Together

Most Christians don't have a good understanding of spiritual gifts. Helping team members understand spiritual gifts is the first step in helping them discover their spiritual gifts. As a team, study passages related to spiritual gifts, such as Romans 12:3-6; 1 Corinthians 12:4-11; Ephesians 4:7-13; 1 Peter 4:10. In addition to studying what the Bible has to say about spiritual gifts, find out what your church's position is on spiritual gifts. Because each church and denomination interprets spiritual gifts slightly differently, it's important for you to know where they stand. Reading such books as *Body Life* by Ray Stedman or *Your Spiritual Gifts Can Help Your Church Grow* by C. Peter Wagner will also expand your understanding of spiritual gifts. A solid understanding of spiritual gifts is a great foundation for helping team members discover their spiritual gifts.

Experiment With Different Ministries

Sometimes the best way to discover your spiritual gifts is to experiment with different opportunities within the ministry. Like most things in life, we learn best by experience and experimentation. Rick Warren shares his thoughts on this topic in *The Purpose-Driven Church*, saying, "Most churches say, 'Discover your spiritual gift and then you'll know what ministry you're supposed to have.' This is backwards. I believe the exact opposite: Start experimenting with different ministries and *then* you'll discover your gifts!"[7]

Give team members the freedom to experiment with different responsibilities within the ministry. One of my volunteers experimented with helping decorate, setting up the youth room, and giving announcements before settling on leading our greeting team. Once she discovered that she had the gift of hospitality, she recognized that welcoming and greeting students was right up her alley. Instead of just trying to get team members to fit in roles where you need them, start helping team members find out where *they fit best*.

> *Instead of just trying to get team members to fit in roles where you need them, start helping team members find out where they fit best.*

Personal Fulfillment

What brings a person fulfillment is another clue to identifying a person's spiritual gifts. Using one's spiritual gifts should bring a sense of satisfaction and enjoyment. God won't give us a spiritual gift that makes us miserable. If doing something brings a person joy and satisfaction, that's a strong indicator that it may be his or her spiritual gift. If someone enjoys working behind the scenes, he or she may have the gift of helps or service. If someone enjoys listening and counseling others, that person may have the gift of encouragement or mercy. If someone enjoys doing all-nighters, he or she may have the gift of martyrdom (just kidding!).

On the flip side, things that frustrate or irritate someone may also be a clue to that person's spiritual gift. For example, if someone tends to be irritated by a lack of organization or structure, that person may have the gift of administration. Or if someone gets frustrated when he or she sees a lack of direction, that person may have the gift of leadership. In the end, helping team members discover what brings them personal fulfillment (as well as what frustrates them) is key to helping them to discover their spiritual gifts.

Administer a Spiritual Gifts Inventory

Spiritual gifts inventories are specific tools designed to help individuals discover their spiritual gifts. The most common spiritual gift inventories are the Wagner-Modified Houts Questionnaire and Trenton Spiritual Gifts Analysis. One difficulty with inventories is that the types of spiritual gifts inventoried as well as the definitions for each gift vary. If you use a spiritual gifts inventory, remember that while it can be a helpful tool, it is by no means a comprehensive or completely accurate way to discover spiritual gifts.

Confirmation From Others

God often uses other Christians to confirm truths in our lives. When it comes to spiritual gifts, we shouldn't be the only ones who recognize them. In *Your Spiritual Gifts Can Help Your Church Grow*, Peter Wagner shares a story about how for several years he thought he had the gift of administration, but when his position came up for confirmation, there was significant disagreement among those evaluating him as to whether administration was his strength. It was only years later that he realized that administration was never his strength or a spiritual gift. As a result, Wagner shares this insight: "The gifts, according to our working definition, are given for use within the context of the Body. It is necessary, then, that other members of the Body have an important say in confirming your gift."[8]

If someone believes he or she has the gift of teaching, but no one else seems to recognize or appreciate it, then maybe it's *not* that person's spiritual gift. On the other hand, if others recognize a person's passion and desire to see others come to Christ, then there's a good chance that evangelism may be his or her spiritual gift. Seeking confirmation from others, especially those that know us best, is an important step in discovering one's spiritual gift.

Spiritual Fruit

The final step to discovering a person's spiritual gifts is seeking out evidence of spiritual fruit. Because God gives spiritual gifts for the purpose of ministry and service, spiritual fruit should be the result of using one's spiritual gift. In *Your Spiritual Gifts Can Help Your Church Grow*, Peter Wagner explains: "If you have the gift of evangelist, people will come to Christ regularly through your ministry. If you have the gift of exhortation, you will help people through their problems and see lives straightened out. If you have the gift of healing, sick people will get well. If you have the gift of administration, the organization will run smoothly. When true gifts are in operation, whatever is supposed to happen will happen."[9]

God confirms spiritual gifts by the fruit that is produced through them. A person can be confident that he or she is exercising a spiritual gift when God blesses others as result of it. I see evidence of this in my youth ministry on a weekly basis as several team members who have the gift of helps bless us every week by coming early and staying late to help set up and clean up the youth room for meetings.

Empower Through Sharing Leadership

Sharing leadership with others plays a large part in empowering team members for ministry. Empowerment is unlikely to happen if a leader isn't willing to share his or her leadership with others. Many leaders resist sharing leadership responsibilities because they're insecure, have a need for control, have a desire for status and power, or are afraid of losing their value. Yet *true leadership* isn't about hoarding authority; it's about giving it away to others. Jesus taught us this principle in Mark 10:45, saying, "For even the Son of Man did not come to be served, but to serve, and to give his life as a ransom for many." If you want to empower others, you need to give them opportunities to share in the leadership. The more ways you can share leadership, the greater you can empower team members. Here are a few practical ways to do this.

Share Information

One of the simplest ways to share leadership is through sharing information. Information is power, and withholding it from team members is a form of control and manipulation. Team members feel excluded and unimportant when information is withheld from them. Sharing information with team members, on the other hand,

Team members feel excluded and unimportant when information is withheld from them.

communicates that we trust them and believe it's important for them to know what is going on. In *The 3 Keys to Empowerment*, Ken Blanchard, John Carlos, and Alan Randolph write, "When leaders are willing to share whatever information they have—both good and bad—they begin to gain the trust of their people, who then feel included and trusted by leadership." Every week at our pastor's meeting, I have the privilege of hearing about all the things that are going on in our church. Instead of being told only positive news about our church, I get to hear the negative news, too. It's empowering for me when those in leadership are willing to include me through trusting me with important information.

Jesus modeled this when he spoke with his disciples about his future betrayal, murder, and resurrection. Mark 10:32b-34 records, "Again he took the Twelve aside and told them what was going to happen to him. 'We are going up to Jerusalem,' he said, 'and the Son of Man will be betrayed to the chief priests and teachers of the law. They will condemn him to death and will hand him over to the Gentiles, who will mock him and spit on him, flog him and kill him. Three days later he will rise.' " Even though they didn't fully understand what he was saying, Jesus chose to empower the disciples by freely sharing this information with them.

While you may not be able to share everything, the more information you can share with your team members, the better. Especially when sharing important information, allow plenty of time for questions and answers. Instead of waiting for the next get-together or scheduling a special meeting, pass information quickly through e-mail, memos, or phone calls. You could even begin sending a weekly e-mail, updating the team with new information relating to the youth ministry. Team members *deserve* to know what's going on. When they're left in the dark, they can end up looking (and feeling) stupid—which is not exactly empowering.

Plan Team Meetings

Team meetings are a simple but often overlooked part of sharing leadership. Many youth ministries that have team meetings fail to structure them in a way that empowers team members. Instead of being a positive and constructive experience, the team meeting becomes a negative and unconstructive time. Ever been to a meeting like this one? The leader does all the talking. The leader makes every decision. Everyone else just tries to passively endure it! Instead of looking forward to the *next* team meeting, team members look forward to the *end* of the meeting. If you want team members to feel empowered, avoid this type of meeting at all costs.

Some youth ministries don't have team meetings at all. Instead of a consistent, regularly scheduled time to meet, the only time team members get together is right before youth group or at a youth event. In *The Team Builder*, Frank Lewis has this to say about the value of team meetings: "If you are going to have a team, you must have a time when the team comes together for a team meeting...The ideal team meeting provides a climate where dreaming, sharpening, focusing, and planning are done in honesty and openness before ministerial peers."

There are lots of reasons why youth workers don't have staff meetings, such as not being willing to plan and think ahead, fear that their team members won't show up, an unwillingness to share information or control with others, or simply not knowing how to run a positive and effective

---

KEYS TO AN EFFECTIVE TEAM MEETING

- Meet regularly (at least once a month).
- Pick a consistent meeting time that works for everyone.
- Before each staff meeting, e-mail or snail mail the agenda to team members.
- Provide time for leaders to share personal updates and prayer requests.
- Encourage feedback and discussion about programs, events, and ideas.
- Involve members in planning, problem-solving, making suggestions, and delegating ministry.
- Put the most important item in the middle, and know what you can cut out if the meeting runs long.
- Keep staff meetings under two hours (unless you are serving food).
- Consider a separate planning meeting for youth calendar events.
- Mail out meeting minutes to absent teammates.

team meeting. Yet teams that fail to come together to share, learn, evaluate, and plan for the ministry easily lose focus and become divided. It becomes only a matter of time before the team feels disorganized and disconnected. Expert team leader and church consultant Harold Westing shares his experience in the *Church Staff Handbook*, saying, "When I find that the relationships of a team are in disarray, I seek to find out if the regular staff meetings are still being held. Most every time, they have discontinued their weekly meetings."[10]

Whether your team meetings are weekly or monthly, the important point is that the team needs to come together on a consistent and regular basis. While every team meeting will have its own personality, it's important that team meetings have the following elements:

- a time for sharing personal needs and prayer requests,
- a time to report what God is doing in and through the ministry,
- a time for training or equipping the team,
- a time for feedback and evaluation of previous events and programs,
- a time for group decision-making and problem-solving, and
- a time for planning and sharing ministry responsibilities.

The following is a sample schedule of one of our team's monthly meetings:

12:30–1:00 p.m. Lunch together

1:00–1:30 p.m. Personal updates and prayer requests

1:30–1:45 p.m. Training focus

1:45–2:15 p.m. Feedback, evaluation, and problem solving

2:15–3:00 p.m. Planning and "calendar-ing"

The goal of a regular structure like this is to make team meetings positive, interactive, and productive. Getting feedback from the team members about meetings is a great way to improve how team meetings are organized. For more helpful ideas, see "Keys to an Effective Team Meeting" (p. 126).

Give Team Members Specific Responsibilities

Especially when a team member begins involvement in the ministry, it's important for him or her to have a specific responsibility in the youth ministry. People feel empowered when they have a role to play, no matter how small that role seems. Doug Fields likes to give this challenge to youth workers: If he were able to instantly give them all the volunteers they needed, would they know how to effectively utilize them? His point is that oftentimes we talk about the need for more volunteers without having really thought through how we would place and use them. Team members that choose to help in the youth ministry but don't have a specific responsibility will eventually feel useless and ineffective. The following are a few examples of specific responsibilities you can give team members:

- helping set up,
- welcoming students,
- leading a game,
- taking prayer requests,
- making announcements,
- leading a small group,
- planning special events,
- teaching Sunday school,
- directing a student ministry team, and
- assisting with the budget or other administrative tasks.

The sooner you can get team members involved by giving them specific responsibilities, the sooner they will feel valued and empowered!

It's also important when giving specific responsibilities to team members to not emphasize tasks at the expense of relationships. Most team members agree to help in the youth ministry because they want to minister to students, not set up chairs. While there is nothing wrong with asking team members to be responsible for specific tasks, the greater goal should always be to empower them to minister powerfully and personally in the lives of students. The faster you connect leaders with students, the more quickly they'll feel empowered. When leaders begin to impact students' lives, their motivation and passion for ministry soars. There is nothing more empowering than knowing that you're making a difference in the life of a young person.

Create Boundaries

Another key to sharing leadership is creating boundaries for team members to work within. In their enthusiasm to empower others, it's a common mistake for leaders to fail to give team members sufficient boundaries in their areas of responsibility. Freedom without boundaries only creates frustration and insecurity. Boundaries should be shaped by the ministry's mission and vision; a boundary is violated if actions, attitudes, and words violate the mission and vision of the ministry.

Boundaries emphasize results, not methods. In other words, boundaries communicate what needs to get done, not necessarily how to do it. Finally, boundaries are influenced by a team member's experience and competence. For example, if a team member leads a game for the first time, you need to give him or her a time frame, available resources, a focus or purpose, and things to avoid. As a team member becomes more competent and experienced, you can increase the boundary lines by giving the person more room to experiment and be innovative. On the other hand, if the team member has led games successfully in the past, you can step back and allow the person to work more on his or her own. It's essential to work closely with team members when giving boundaries because each person will have different needs and concerns. Because boundaries are dynamic and ever-changing, it's important to modify them when needed. Empowerment results when team members are given positive and reasonable boundaries to carry out their ministry responsibilities.

Empowerment results when team members are given positive and reasonable boundaries to carry out their ministry responsibilities.

Provide Accountability

The final key to sharing leadership is providing accountability. As much as we would like to ignore accountability, it's an essential part of leadership. Kenn Gangel in *Coaching Ministry Teams* describes it this way: "In accountability we do not let go of people, we let go of power. When we delegate both responsibility and authority, we still have the responsibility to maintain accountability, holding people to achieve what they agreed to do."[11] Accountability works to make sure that progress is being made and that the team members are working within their boundaries. A lack of accountability almost always results in loss of effectiveness. In *Empowered Leaders*, Hans Finzel shares how he had to learn about the value of accountability the hard way: "I probably trust people too much; nine times out of ten I am overly optimistic about their productivity potential. However, I've also found that the reality of human nature is that people do what you inspect more than what you expect. So you have to build in some means of checking on the progress of the work."[12]

Accountability is not to be confused with micromanaging or looking over people's shoulders. Instead, accountability is an opportunity for team members to receive support, feedback, and guidance. Accountability should be a positive experience for everyone involved. Providing accountability for team members means taking time to listen, keeping updated on their progress, and encouraging and challenging them to a higher level.

Some team members will require more accountability than others. Team members who need the least amount of accountability tend to be self-directed and self-motivated. They need very few reminders, and if they need help, they will come to you instead of you having to come to them. Team members who need the most accountability will often wait until someone checks on them before starting a project. They need lots of reminders, and when they run into a problem, they are more likely to wait for you to initiate help. As you get to know your team members, you'll soon discover their unique needs. Tailor your accountability style to meet individual team members' needs.

Conclusion

Jesus was the ultimate empowerer. Even though he was the most powerful person in the universe, Jesus freely shared his power and authority with others. Even in his final hours on earth, Jesus empowered his disciples: "Then Jesus came to them and said, 'All authority in heaven and on earth has been given to me. Therefore go and make disciples of all nations, baptizing them in the name of the Father and of the Son and of the Holy Spirit, and teaching them to obey everything I have commanded you. And surely I am with you always, to the very end of the age' " (Matthew 28:18-20).

To live for Christ is to be empowered by him. The Great Commission isn't so much about evangelism as it is about Christians being empowered by Christ to change the world. Investing in others, helping people discover their gifts and abilities, and sharing leadership were unmistakable characteristics of Jesus' life and ministry. To be like Jesus means empowering those around you to become all that God desires for them to be.

NOW WHAT?

1. On a scale of one to ten (ten being the best), how would you rate your ability to empower others?

2. What are "safe" and "positive" ways you can allow team members to fail?

3. Schedule a "personal goals" meeting with each team member.

4. Do a Bible study with your team on understanding and discovering spiritual gifts.

5. Have team members take a spiritual gifts inventory.

6. Find efficient and effective ways to share information with team members.

7. Make a list of all the possible responsibilities within the ministry.

8. Create a positive approach to keeping team members accountable.

Team-Builder Questions

1. Share a personal experience of being empowered by someone.

2. How does empowerment differ from delegation and training?

3. What are appropriate and inappropriate situations of allowing others to fail?

4. What do you see as your spiritual gifts, and how are they best expressed on the team?

5. What are ways we can improve how we share information with each other?

6. How can we make our team meetings more productive and beneficial?

7. What specific responsibilities can we divide up among team members?

ENDNOTES

1. *Leading the Team-Based Church,* George Cladis, copyright © 1999 George Cladis. Reprinted by permission of John Wiley & Sons, Inc.

2. Excerpted from *Building Strong People* by Bobbie Reed and John Westfall, copyright © 1997 Network of Single Adult Leaders. Reprinted by permission of Dr. John Westfall.

3. Excerpted from *Building Strong People* by Bobbie Reed and John Westfall, copyright © 1997 Network of Single Adult Leaders. Reprinted by permission of Dr. John Westfall.

4. *Empowered Leaders,* Hans Finzel, copyright © 1998, W Publishing Group, Nashville, Tennessee. All rights reserved.

5. *Coaching Ministry Teams,* Kenn Gangel, copyright © 2000, W Publishing Group, Nashville, Tennessee. All rights reserved.

6. *Doing Church as a Team* by Wayne Cordeiro. Copyright © 2001. Regal Books, Ventura, CA 93003. Used by permission.

7. Taken from *The Purpose-Driven Church* by Rick Warren. Copyright © 1995 by Rick Warren. Used by permission of Zondervan.

8. *Your Spiritual Gifts Can Help Your Church Grow* by C. Peter Wagner. Copyright © 1979, 1994. Regal Books, Ventura, CA 93003. Used by permission.

9. *Your Spiritual Gifts Can Help Your Church Grow* by C. Peter Wagner. Copyright © 1979, 1994. Regal Books, Ventura, CA 93003. Used by permission.

10. Taken from *Church Staff Handbook* © 1985, 1997 by Harold J. Westing. Published by Kregel Publications, Grand Rapids, MI. Used by permission. All rights reserved.

11. *Coaching Ministry Teams,* Kenn Gangel, copyright © 2000, W Publishing Group, Nashville, Tennessee. All rights reserved.

12. *Empowered Leaders,* Hans Finzel, copyright © 1998, W Publishing Group, Nashville, Tennessee. All rights reserved.

"Coming together is a beginning,
keeping together is progress,
and working together is success."
HENRY FORD

"A man injured on the job filed an insurance claim. The insurance company requested more information, so the man wrote the insurance company the following letter of explanation:

Dear Sirs:

I am writing in response to your request concerning clarification of the information I supplied in block #11 on the insurance form, which asked for the cause of the injury. I answered, 'Trying to do the job alone.' I trust that the following explanation will be sufficient.

I am a bricklayer by trade. On the date of the injury, I was working alone, laying brick around the top of a three-story building. When I finished the job, I had about five hundred pounds of brick left over. Rather than carry the bricks down by hand, I decided to put them into a barrel and lower them by a pulley that was fastened to the top of the building.

I secured the end of the rope at ground level, went back up to the top of the building, loaded the bricks into the barrel, and pushed it over the side. I then went back down to the ground and untied the rope, holding it securely to insure the slow descent of the barrel. As you will note in block #6 of the insurance form, I weigh 145 pounds. At the shock of being jerked off the ground so swiftly by the five hundred pounds of bricks in the barrel, I lost my presence of mind and forgot to let go of the rope.

Between the second and third floors I met the barrel. This accounts for the bruises and lacerations on my upper body. Fortunately, I retained enough presence of mind to maintain my tight hold on the rope and proceeded rapidly up the side of the building, not stopping until my right hand was jammed in the pulley. This accounts for my broken thumb (see block #4). Despite the pain, I continued to hold tightly to the rope. Unfortunately, at approximately the same time, the barrel hit the ground and the bottom fell out of the barrel. Devoid of the weight of the bricks, the barrel now weighed about fifty pounds. I again refer you to block #6, where my weight is listed. I began a rapid descent.

In the vicinity of the second floor, I met the barrel coming up. This explains the injury to my legs and lower body. Slowed only slightly, I continued my descent, landing on the pile of bricks. Fortunately, my back was only sprained. I am sorry to report, however, that at this point I again lost my presence of mind—and let go of the rope.

I trust that this answers your concern. Please note that I am finished trying to do the job alone." (From *Hot Illustrations for Youth Talks* by Wayne Rice)[1]

Unlike the bricklayer who had to learn the hard way, we have the opportunity to learn from those who've gone before us. The writer of Ecclesiastes understood the importance of sharing ministry with others, writing, "Two are better than one, because they have a good return for their work: If one falls down, his friend can help him up. But pity the man who falls and has no one to help him up! Also, if two lie down together, they will keep warm. But how can one keep warm alone? Though one may be overpowered, two can defend themselves. A cord of three strands is not quickly broken" (Ecclesiastes 4:9-12). Ministry was *never* meant to be a one-person show; God intends it to be a team effort. As you prepare to lead a team-centered youth ministry, keep the following things in mind.

Lead by Example

Like many things in life, teamwork is more caught than taught. People are more apt to follow the leader's example than the leader's words. If you as the leader are not clearly and visibly modeling teamwork for others, then it's unlikely that teamwork will ever develop. If you're still making all the decisions and not allowing others to influence the ministry, then the need for control (not teamwork) is being modeled. If you're taking all the attention and credit for the ministry, self-centeredness (not humility) is being modeled. If you're asking team members to make sacrifices while at the same time refusing to make the same sacrifices, hypocrisy (not self-sacrifice) is being modeled. In order for teamwork to be

Like many things in life, teamwork is more caught than taught.

contagious, it needs to be powerfully demonstrated in a leader's life.

When I arrived at my current church, I had to work extra hard at modeling teamwork because of the previous reputation of the youth ministry. Wanting to be seen as team-oriented, I tried to find as many ways as possible to model to others that the youth ministry valued teamwork and cooperating with others. The thing that helped most was sharing a very successful fund-raiser event with other ministries. In the past, the youth auction had raised large amounts of money and provided high visibility for the youth ministry. But while it had been a successful event for the youth ministry, it created inequality for other ministries that didn't have a comparable event. After doing the auction the first year, I decided to open it up to other ministries the following year. Even though I received some criticism for doing this, I felt it was the right thing to do. The good news is that it paid off and we had the largest and most successful auction ever. And the best part is that instead of seeing the youth ministry as self-focused and independent, other ministry leaders began seeing us as team-oriented and supportive.

Jesus modeled this principle powerfully in John 13 when he washed his disciples' feet as an example of the servanthood he taught them about. Unlike Jesus, many leaders get excited about teamwork but fail to model it in their lives. Because actions always speak louder than words, leaders need to make sure they model what they teach.

Understand Team Development

Also keep in mind that teams go through different stages of development. Like any group, teams move through various stages as they become more connected and committed to God's purposes. Leaders make a fatal mistake when they expect their teams to transform overnight. Understanding the various stages and the different styles of leadership required will be helpful to you as you lead your team.

STAGE 1: Excitement

The excitement stage usually occurs when a team first comes together. There's a lot of enthusiasm and energy as the team is formed, but there's not yet much direction or purpose for the group. Members aren't clear on their roles or the exact function of the team. The leader's role is to help bring focus to the team by clarifying goals, addressing expectations, and providing opportunities for the team members to get to know each other. In the excitement stage, the leader takes a more directive role as he or she moves the team forward to the next stage.

STAGE 2: Adjustment

Having moved through the excitement stage, the team now moves into the adjustment stage. In this stage, teams are getting accustomed to each other and their different roles. There is a certain degree of ambiguity as team members are figuring out what is and isn't acceptable. The leader's role at this stage is to help the team arrive at mutually agreeable behaviors and expectations. The most common way to do this is by helping the team develop a team covenant as described in Chapter 6. Unlike the excitement stage in which the leader gives most of the direction, the leader is now focused on helping the team arrive at an agreement of expectations and objectives.

STAGE 3: Conflict

In the conflict stage, the team members are now becoming open and honest with each other. As team members feel more comfortable with each other and with expressing their personal opinions and ideas, conflict is free to surface. Conflict can result from misunderstandings, personality differences, or unmet expectations. This conflict is a necessary and healthy component of any team, and if dealt with correctly, it will help the team become stronger. The leader's role is to help the team address the various conflicts and encourage team members to resolve them positively. Evaluating team practices and making adjustments are vital parts of the leader's role.

STAGE 4: Performance

If a team successfully moves through the conflict stage, the next stage is the performance stage—the stage at which the team is operating at peak efficiency. The team is unified and focused. Committed to supporting and strengthening each other, team members are ready to give the team their all. Everyone understands his or her role and is committed to the team's mission, vision, and goals. The leader moves from directing the team to empowering the team. Sharing ministry and helping team members become successful are now top priorities for the leader.

Understanding the stages of team development will be a useful tool in helping you lead your team. When the team gets stuck in a specific stage, your role is to assist the team in moving to the next stage by helping overcome the obstacles and differences.

Practice Makes Perfect

Early on in college, I had gotten the bug to be an emergency medical technician (EMT). An EMT is someone who works on an ambulance and responds to all sorts of emergencies. Feeling highly motivated, I signed up for an EMT class that involved over 700 pages of reading on emergency care, 120 hours of classroom instruction, and an eight-hour ambulance ride at the end of class. After passing the class with flying colors, I felt totally prepared to work as an EMT.

After dropping off a few résumés and going through a few interviews, I landed a job at a local ambulance company. I was so excited that I could barely sleep the night before my first shift. I imagined driving up to an emergency scene and confidently knowing what to do and where to go. I imagined everyone complimenting me on how much of a natural I was. Unfortunately, reality didn't meet my imagination. The next day was a total and complete disaster. Rather than knowing what to do, I got nervous and became confused. It was a miracle that I even made it through my first shift! Instead of being told I was a natural, I was told that I couldn't get any worse. I learned a valuable lesson that day that knowledge and experience are two entirely different things. The

> *I learned a valuable lesson that day that knowledge and experience are two entirely different things.*

goods news is that as I gained more experience, I eventually became a capable and competent EMT.

While you've gained a lot of knowledge about developing a team-centered youth ministry, the next step is to put it into practice. Knowledge should complement, not replace, experience. Instead of being an end unto itself, knowledge should be a starting point for effective ministry. While you won't be able to implement everything at once, it's critical that you develop a plan of how to put into practice what you've learned. After all, practice makes perfect.

Be Patient

The final thing to keep in mind is to be patient. Good things don't happen overnight. Although we live in a world that seeks instant gratification, when it comes to developing a team-centered youth ministry, realize that it won't happen as quickly as you would like. Consider Jesus' ministry with his disciples. Having spent three long years with them, sharing almost every experience and opportunity for growth and ministry, it wasn't until after he left that they began to demonstrate true teamwork. If it took Jesus over three years to see teamwork finally develop, we can't expect to do it faster! It's not that progress won't be made along the way, but expecting your team to transform within a year is unrealistic and unlikely. Even at my current ministry, I have yet to see all the things discussed in this book become reality. While I've seen them developed in other ministries I've led, I've needed to be patient as I laid the groundwork for a team-centered youth ministry.

Patience means doing your part and allowing God to do his. Too often because of impatience, we try to make everything happen on our timetables and not God's. Rather than letting God be God, we try to take control and force things to happen. Because there are many things in our ministries that are out of our control, the sooner we give them over to God, the sooner he can begin taking control. Sharing his own journey, Doug Fields writes, "I realized that, ultimately, programs don't work—God works. God doesn't need a program in order to work. He doesn't even need me. This realization brought humility when I finally admitted my very small part in God's work. When good things happen I need to recognize that they happen because of God's power and not my own."[2]

Work hard, pray hard, and then be patient as God does his thing. And last of all, remember that we serve a mighty God. "Now to him who is able to do immeasurably more than all we ask or imagine, according to his power that is at work within us, to him be glory in the church and in Christ Jesus throughout all generations, for ever and ever! Amen" (Ephesians 3:20-21).

NOW WHAT?

1. What are ways you can model teamwork and cooperation to others?

2. What stage is your team currently in?

3. What steps can you take in order to help move the team to the next stage?

4. Type up a plan detailing how you will begin moving toward a team-centered youth ministry.

5. When you feel impatient, spend time in prayer releasing the ministry to God.

Team-Builder Questions

1. In what ways can you identify with the bricklayer trying to do the job alone?

2. What are practical ways we can lead by example through modeling teamwork to others?

3. What stage best describes our team development?

4. What needs to happen in order to move our team into the next stage?

5. What area(s) in our ministry is God calling us to actively pursue?

6. What area(s) in our ministry is God calling us to wait on him about?

ENDNOTES

1. Reprinted from *Hot Illustrations for Youth Talks*, copyright © 1994 by Youth Specialties, Inc., 300 South Pierce Street, El Cajon, CA 92020. www.YouthSpecialties.com. Used by permission.
2. Taken from *Purpose-Driven™ Youth Ministry* by Doug Fields. Copyright © 1998 by Doug Fields. Used by permission of Zondervan.

Here are some great resources that may be helpful to you as you continue to develop a team-centered youth ministry.

Leadership

The 21 Irrefutable Laws of Leadership by John C. Maxwell (Nashville, TN: Thomas Nelson, 1998)

Becoming a Person of Influence by John C. Maxwell and Jim Dornan (Nashville, TN: Thomas Nelson, 1997)

Developing a Vision for Ministry in the 21st Century by Aubrey Malphurs (Grand Rapids, MI: Baker Book House, 1999)

Doing Church as a Team by Wayne Cordeiro (Ventura, CA: Regal Books, 2001)

Empowered Leaders by Hans Finzel (Nashville, TN: W Publishing Group, 1998)

Your Spiritual Gifts Can Help Your Church Grow by C. Peter Wagner (Ventura, CA: Regal Books, 1994)

Personal Growth

Fresh Wind, Fresh Fire by Jim Cymbala (Grand Rapids, MI: Zondervan Publishing House, 1997)

The Godbearing Life by Kenda Creasy Dean and Ron Foster (Nashville, TN: Upper Room Books, 1998)

Spiritual Leadership by J. Oswald Sanders (Chicago, IL: Moody Press, 1994)

Understanding How Others Misunderstand You by Ken Voges and Ron Braund (Chicago, IL: Moody Press, 1995)

Visioneering by Andy Stanley (Sisters, OR: Multnomah Publishers, Inc., 1999)

General Youth Ministry

Family-Based Youth Ministry by Mark DeVries (Downers Grove, IL: InterVarsity Press, 1994)

Help! I'm a Volunteer Youth Worker! by Doug Fields (Grand Rapids, MI: Zondervan Publishing House/Youth Specialties, 1993)

Purpose-Driven™ Youth Ministry by Doug Fields (Grand Rapids, MI: Zondervan Publishing House/Youth Specialties, 1998)

The Youth Builder by Jim Burns, Ph.D. and Mike DeVries (Ventura, CA: Gospel Light, 2001)

Discipleship

The Ministry of Nurture by Duffy Robbins (Grand Rapids, MI: Zondervan Publishing House/Youth Specialties, 1990)

Shaping the Spiritual Lives of Students by Richard R. Dunn (Downers Grove, IL: InterVarsity Press, 2001)

Evangelism

The Battle for a Generation by Ron Hutchcraft (Chicago, IL: Moody Press, 1996)

Becoming a Contagious Christian Youth Edition by Mark Mittelberg, Lee Strobel, and Bill Hybels (Grand Rapids, MI: Zondervan Publishing House, 2001)

Contagious Faith by Dave Rahn and Terry Linhart (Loveland, CO: Group Publishing, Inc., 2000)

Jesus for a New Generation by Kevin Graham Ford (Downers Grove, IL: InterVarsity Press, 1995)

The Master's Plan for Making Disciples by Win and Charles Arn (Grand Rapids, MI: Baker Book House, 1998)

Youth Culture

Post-Modern Pilgrims by Leonard Sweet (Nashville, TN: Broadman & Holman Publishers, 2000)

Real Teens by George Barna (Ventura, CA: Regal Books, 2001)

Trendwatch by Rick Lawrence (Loveland, CO: Group Publishing, Inc., 2000)

Understanding Today's Youth Culture by Walt Mueller (Carol Stream, IL: Tyndale House Publishers, 1999)

Small Groups

Get 'Em Talking! by Mike Yaconelli and Scott Koenigsaecker (Grand Rapids, MI: Zondervan Publishing House/Youth Specialties, 1989)

Hear Me Out Cards (Volumes I and II) by Bill Muir (Denver, CO: YFC/Creative Youth Resources, 2001)

Help! I'm a Small-Group Leader by Laurie Polich (Grand Rapids, MI: Zondervan Publishing House/Youth Specialties, 1998)

How to Lead Small Groups by Neil F. McBride (Colorado Springs, CO: NavPress, 1990)

EVALUATION FOR

No More Lone Rangers

Please help Group Publishing, Inc., continue to provide innovative and useful resources for ministry. Please take a moment to fill out this evaluation and mail or fax it to us. Thanks!

Group Publishing, Inc.
Attention: Product Development
P.O. Box 481
Loveland, CO 80539
Fax: (970) 679-4370

1. As a whole, this book has been (circle one)
   not very helpful   *very helpful*
   1   2   3   4   5   6   7   8   9   10

2. The best things about this book:

3. Ways this book could be improved:

4. Things I will change because of this book:

5. Other books I'd like to see Group publish in the future:

6. Would you be interested in field-testing future Group products and giving us your feedback? If so, please fill in the information below:

Name_____

Church Name _____

Denomination _____ Church Size _____

Church Address _____

City _____ State_____ ZIP _____

Church Phone _____

E-mail _____

Powerful Resources for Connecting With Youth!

City Lights:
Ministry Essentials for Reaching Urban Youth

Scott Larson and Karen Free, General Editors

You're a Christ-modeling bridge-builder… committed to bringing urban youth of all types together as the body of Christ. And whatever your experience in urban youth ministry, you'll need to gear up. *City Lights* will give you essential strategies to be effective. You'll find the most cutting-edge urban youth ministry models in practice today. And they're brought to you by authors who've served on the front-lines. Every aspect of this complex, yet rewarding, ministry is covered in 18 chapters!

Scott Larson is president of Straight Ahead Ministries, which he co-founded with his wife, Hanne. Straight Ahead operates Bible studies in numerous juvenile detention centers, provides aftercare mentoring programs and discipleship homes. This is his latest project. He has authored four books, including At Risk: Bringing Hope to Hurting Teenagers, *and* Risk in Our Midst: Empowering Teenagers to Love the Unlovable.

Karen Free is director of communications for Straight Ahead Ministries, Inc. She has spent the last thirty years in print media as a newspaper reporter, freelance writer, journalist, and editor.

ISBN 0-7644-2386-X

Flagship church resources
from Group Publishing

The Winning Spirit:
Empowering Teenagers Through God's Grace

Chris Hill

This youth ministry veteran details a fresh vision and practical philosophy for youth ministry. It's about loving kids as Jesus loves them. Grace-based youth ministry that gives students a God's-eye view of themselves, as winners. Be inspired, encouraged, and motivated by a new dream for your youth ministry.

Chris Hill is an 18-year youth ministry veteran of successful grace-based youth ministry in both urban and suburban settings. A sought-after speaker and writer, he currently serves as youth pastor for The Potter's House in Dallas, Texas, where Bishop T.D. Jakes serves as pastor—the largest African-American church in the country.

ISBN 0-7644-2396-7